INVESTMENT STRATEGIES
AND THE PLANT-LOCATION DECISION

INVESTMENT STRATEGIES AND THE PLANT–LOCATION DECISION
FOREIGN COMPANIES IN THE UNITED STATES

Robert W. Haigh

with the assistance of
Richard A. Adams,
Clark A. Driftmier, and
Teresa K. Welch

New York
Westport, Connecticut
London

Copyright Acknowledgments

The author acknowledges the use of excerpts from *Buying Into America* by Martin and Susan Tolchin. Copyright 1987 by Martin and Susan Tolchin. Reprinted by permission of Times Books, a Division of Random House, Inc.

Library of Congress Cataloging-in-Publication Data

Haigh, Robert William, 1926-
    Investment strategies and the plant-location decision.

    Includes bibliographical references.
    1. Business enterprises, Foreign—United States—Location. 2. Corporations, Foreign—United States. 3. Industries—United States—Location. 4. Investments, Foreign—United States. I. Title.
HC110.D5H35 1989   338.8'8873   89-22975
ISBN 0-275-93344-X (alk. paper)

Library of Congress Catalog Card Number: 89-22975
ISBN: 0-275-93344-X

First published in 1989

Praeger Publishers, One Madison Avenue, New York, NY 10010
A division of Greenwood Press, Inc.

Printed in the United States of America

∞

The paper used in this book complies with the Permanent Paper Standard issued by the National Information Standards Organization (Z39.48—1984).

10 9 8 7 6 5 4 3 2 1

CONTENTS

Participate in the U.S. Market. Improve Customer Service. Implement Product Strategies. Attain Advertising and Promotion Objectives. Maintain Customer Service by International Expansion. Enhance Cost Competitiveness. Hedge Foreign Currency Exchange Fluctuations. Develop a Global Strategy. Achieve Profitability and Return-On-Investment Objectives.

Technology and Plant Equipment. Decentralized Management Philosophy. Managerial and Technical Personnel Policies. Export Strategies. Compensation Policies. Corporate Image. Procurement. Union Attitude.

TABLES

FIGURES

PREFACE

This project was initiated in the spring of 1988 as one of the early research undertakings of the Tayloe Murphy International Business Studies Center, a research agency affiliated with the Darden Graduate School of Business Administration at the University of Virginia.

There is considerable interest in the questions:

Why do foreign companies establish manufacturing operations in the United States?

How do the managements of these companies decide on the specific U.S. locations for their plants?

The research was undertaken in the hope that the findings might be of interest and benefit to five principal audiences:

- managements of foreign companies who are considering and evaluating the establishment of U.S. manufacturing operations

- economic development professionals in state, regional, or local agencies and directors of chambers of commerce who persuade and assist foreign companies in their plant location decisions

- public policymakers (legislators and state, county, and city officials) who have a deep interest in attracting new investments

- domestic business executives who may be watching the arrival of new competition from abroad with mixed feelings

- academicians who have developed a considerable body of knowledge concerning the theory and practice involved in foreign direct investment and plant-investment decisions.

This publication was made possible by the helpful and enthusiastic cooperation of executives in twenty U.S. affiliates or subsidiaries of foreign companies. In all but a few cases, the executives we interviewed had been directly involved in the investment and plant location decisions under review. The principal corporate executives and economic development officials participating in the study are shown on Table P.1. One company that joined in the study is not listed, since the management decided to maintain anonymity. We are grateful for the kind treatment afforded us by everyone who assisted us.

Three research assistants contributed heavily to the research effort. A considerable contribution was made by Richard Adams and Clark Driftmier, second-year students in the MBA program at the Darden School. They helped with the company contact work and did much of the research relating to plant-location factors and foreign direct investment (FDI). Teresa Welch is a full-time research assistant at the Tayloe Murphy Center. She conducted an extensive literature search, provided helpful background on the foreign direct investment material, and edited the manuscript.

We are appreciative of the substantial support given by Henry Wingate and his associates at the Darden School Library and by the library staff personnel of the Government Documents Department at Alderman Library at the University of Virginia. Also, we are grateful for the careful editing and constructive suggestions made by Bette Collins, Research Editor at the Darden School.

Evelyn Carpenter typed the manuscript, tables, and figures and, using desktop publishing technology, did an excellent job producing "camera-ready" copy for publication. She also maintained liaisons with the company participants and helped with the editing. Her patience and enthusiasm are appreciated by all of us.

The sponsor of this study, the Tayloe Murphy International Business Studies Center, was formed in September, 1987. The Center conducts broad-based research on international business topics for academicians, business practitioners, and public policymakers. In addition, it undertakes sponsored research projects to assist specific businesses in the implementation of their foreign trade and investment initiatives. The Center provides direction for the enrichment of study programs in international business, including the design of executive development programs.

The keen interest and constant support of Leslie E. Grayson, Director of the Center, are acknowledged with deep appreciation. Our thanks is also extended to members of the business community whose donations helped to fund the study.

I am grateful for the support provided by everyone mentioned above. In the final analysis, however, the complete responsibility for the final document, including all of the findings and conclusions, is mine.

Darden Graduate School
of Business Administration,
University of Virginia

ROBERT W. HAIGH
Distinguished Professor
of Business Administration

Table P.1
STUDY PARTICIPANTS
COMPANIES

ALLIED COLLOIDS INC.
Paul Beaulieu, General Manager

BARBOURSVILLE VINEYARDS
Adriano Rossi, Manager and Winemaker

CANON VIRGINIA, INC.
Tadao Okabe, Director

D-SCAN, INC.
Robert Keith, Plant Manager

**ERNI COMPONENTS DIVISION OF
ODIN COMPONENTS, INC.**
Willy Rau, Vice President, Production

FIORUCCI FOODS CORPORATION
Claudio Colmignoli, President

Felix T. Garcia, Director of Purchasing
and Materials Management

**FRANZ HAAS MACHINERY
OF AMERICA, INC.**
Bernhard B. Barta, General Manager

G. D PACKAGE MACHINERY INC.
Giuseppe Venturi,
Executive Vice President, Operations

HERMLE BLACK FOREST CLOCKS
Helmut Mangold, Plant Manager

INTERTAPE, INC.
Howard Simpson, Plant Manager

LINGUANOTO, INC.
Andre Lau-Hansen, President

NEW ALBERENE STONE CO.
Pentti Martikainen, President

OPTON, INC.
Masako Tatsuguchi, President

SAN-J INTERNATIONAL
Stephen J. Earle, Vice President,
International Operations

Mark R. Givens, Vice President
and General Manager

**SUMITOMO MACHINERY
CORPORATION OF AMERICA**
Gary Combs,
Marketing Manager

VDO-YAZAKI CORPORATION
Colleen Bly, Director of
Human Resources

VSL CORPORATION
Steven Parsick, Controller

WALTER GRINDERS
Paris Kazee, Controller

WEIDMULLER INC.
Wolfgang V. Schubl, President

ECONOMIC DEVELOPMENT AGENCIES

FORWARD HAMPTON ROADS
Gregory H. Wingfield, President

Ann J. Baldwin, Director of Research

**INDUSTRIAL DEVELOPMENT
AUTHORITY OF LOUISA COUNTY**
Peter O. Ward, Coordinator

**NORTH CAROLINA DEPARTMENT
OF COMMERCE**
Robert G. Brinkley, Assistant Director,
Business/Industry Development Division

E. Ray Denny, International Division

Gary L. Shope,
Senior Economic Developer

**VIRGINIA DEPARTMENT OF
ECONOMIC DEVELOPMENT**
Hugh Keogh, Director

Mark Kilduff, Deputy Director,
Industrial Development

Evelyn Glazier, Director,
Marketing Services

Paul H. Grossman, Jr., Analyst,
International Marketing

Terry W. Lentz, Manager,
International Marketing

Roger McCauley, Director,
International Marketing

Robert F. Morse, Manager,
International Marketing

INVESTMENT STRATEGIES
AND THE PLANT–LOCATION DECISION

PART 1

BACKGROUND

In addition to providing some background on foreign direct investment (FDI) in the United States, this part summarizes the literature on both FDI theory and on the plant–location decision process. This part also describes the research methodology used in this study.

Foreign direct manufacturing investments are a growing and visible part of the U.S. manufacturing scene. The number of foreign–owned companies, the number of foreign–owned plants, the size of foreign investments in the United States, and the proportion of Americans working for foreign–owned companies are growing steadily. Canadian, British, West German, Japanese, Swiss, French, and Dutch companies have been particularly active in making plant investments in the United States, and foreign manufacturing facilities are represented in all leading U.S. industries. These trends, which are discussed in some detail in the appendix, result from a multitude of investment decisions by individual companies. After a decision to invest in the United States has been made, foreign managements make their plant–location decisions. Because of the favorable economic benefits associated with new plant investments, most states and many communities are intensely interested in this process, and they compete aggressively for the foreign plant investments. This study describes the processes at work in the decisions to invest in the United States and in the location of plants.

The encouragement of FDI in the United States is not without controversy. The controversy is described by Martin and Susan Tolchin in their book *Buying Into America: How Foreign Money is Changing the Face of Our Nation.* According to the authors, pro–investment enthusiasm is exemplified by former Tennessee Governor Lamar Alexander. Between 1980 and 1986, Governor Alexander made six promotional trips to Japan. He wrote a book entitled *Friends*, outlining the reasons so many people and companies from Japan have located in Tennessee, and during the years of his administration, Tennessee outstripped all other states in the amount of Japanese manufacturing investments.

The anti–investment sentiment, according to the Tolchins, is exhibited by the posture of Richard Lamm, former governor of Colorado. Lamm warned:

I do not want Japanese coming in and buying up American technology. I do not want them in our state [Colorado]. I don't want the Arabs owning our banks or the Japanese owning our means of production. It terrifies me.

However, Roy Romer, Lamm's successor as governor of Colorado, began his administration by adopting a pro–investment posture. He appointed an economic development director to a cabinet–level post, and he headed a delegation of development officials and prominent businessmen on a trip to Tokyo to encourage Japanese investment in Colorado (Martin and Susan Tolchin, 1988).

The interest in direct manufacturing investments by foreign companies in the United States sparked this study's several research objectives:

- to acquire insights into the nature, character, and strategies of the foreign companies that are moving to the United States

- to develop an understanding of the reasons foreign firms establish manufacturing operations in the United States

- to gain insights into the managerial process or reasoning by which foreign companies make their plant–location decisions in this country

- to uncover any major problems encountered by the participating companies, thereby providing useful information to executives of companies contemplating U.S. operations

FOREIGN DIRECT INVESTMENT THEORY AND RESEARCH

A considerable body of theoretical and empirical research has explored the motivation for FDI. While this study was not designed to assess the validity of any specific theory, a theoretical background is provided here because many of the companies we surveyed cited reasons for investing in the United States that are consistent with the findings of other researchers.

Much of the theory is designed to explain why exporters are led to make manufacturing investments abroad. Early theories explaining the motivation for FDI focused on the the existence of various market imbalances, such as differences among countries in corporate profitability, currency values, and the cost of labor or capital (Calvet, 1981). More recently, however, less emphasis has been placed on these factors as direct causes of foreign investment; instead, they have been treated more as underlying conditions that can influence a firm to make a foreign investment, but only when other factors such as marketing or technological advantages are also present in such a move.

Surveys of foreign companies in the United States have found that cost factors play a significant role in the decision to establish manufacturing facilities here

(Ajami and Ricks, 1981; Kahley, 1987). Attempts to verify the importance of these factors statistically, however, have yielded mixed results. For example, Caves (1974) found that differences in labor costs showed some significance in explaining foreign investment in Canada but not in the United Kingdom.

Other authors have hypothesized that trade barriers may play a role in motivating FDI, by raising the cost of exporting to a protected market and making the alternative of local production more attractive (Calvet, 1981). Numerous authors have attempted to verify the hypothesis, but again, results have been mixed. Surveys by Daniels (1971), McClain (1983), and the U.S. Department of Commerce (1973, 1976) found that firms often cited trade barriers as a reason for investing in the United States. Moreover, Lall and Siddharthan (1982) did find a correlation between tariffs and FDI in the United States. Neither these authors nor Caves (1974), however, found any statistical relationship between tariff levels and investment abroad by U.S. or foreign corporations. One should note that all these studies used rather rudimentary approximations to measure trade barriers, such as average tariff levels. The approximations ignored both the importance of nontariff barriers to trade and the possibility that foreign investment may be prompted more by changes in the levels of trade barriers than by the existing barriers themselves.

In the 1970s, a number of FDI theories centered on the investment process in oligopolistic industries — industries or markets in which each of a few manufacturers is strong enough to influence the total market by pricing or other actions but not strong enough to disregard reactions by competitors. The theories concern certain competitive and other actions of firms in these industries Some theories focused on the responses of these firms to overseas investments by competitors. Knickerbocker (1974), for example, hypothesized that foreign investment by one firm would trigger investment by rival firms, because rivals would be concerned that entry into a new market by the first firm would upset global market shares or competitive balances among all firms in the industry. There would also be a concern that the initial investor might gain an advantage in terms of market knowledge or competitive options. In testing this hypothesis about oligopolistic industries, Knickerbocker studied the U.S. investments of 372 Canadian and European firms. In each U.S. industry, he found a strong tendency for follow–on investments to be made in clumps after the initial investment had been made.

A similar theory was proposed by Graham (1978), who believed that European firms invested in the United States for two reasons: they were responding to U.S. investments by European competitors, and they were trying to counter any advantages that U.S. companies may have gained from their investments in Europe. In this exchange–of–threat scenario, rivals invade each other's markets to maintain overall global market shares. In addition to Graham, Knickerbocker (1974) and Flowers (1976) found a significant correlation between the dates of U.S. investments in Europe and dates of subsequent investments by Europeans in the United States.

Hymer (1960 and 1976), Kindleberger (1969), and Caves (1971) focused on other characteristics of oligopolies as explanations for foreign investment. To compete successfully overseas, they pointed out, foreign firms must overcome inherent advantages enjoyed by domestic firms, such as greater familiarity with the local market. According to Caves and others, the ability of a foreign firm to distinguish its product in some way from similar products of overseas competitors is the most likely way to gain such an advantage. A multinational company would then be in a position to convince consumers that its product was in some way superior to locally produced products.

The product differentiation concept is broad enough to include also such firm-specific advantages as special marketing skills or technological knowledge. These firm–specific advantages are referred to as intangible assets. The advantages gained from product differentiation are most likely to occur in oligopolistic industries. Once product differentiation is established, new, unknown firms are less likely to enter the market (Caves, 1971; Horst, 1972; Calvet, 1981).

Numerous studies have been conducted to analyze the relationship between the intangible assets held by companies and their foreign investments. Most of these studies deal with foreign investment by U.S. companies, although, in recent years, investment in the United States by foreign firms has received attention as well. In most cases, researchers have used levels of research and advertising expenditures as the indicators of intangible assets.

Several authors have found a relationship between the foreign investments of U.S. companies in various industries and their expenditures for research and development (Horst, 1972; Caves, 1974; Severn, 1974; Grubaugh, 1987). If the relationship was not studied on an industry–by–industry basis, however, no correlation was found. That is, the amount of foreign investment by companies in all industries was not correlated with the amount of their research and advertising expenditures (Horst, 1972).

There is even less certainty whether intangible assets explain foreign investment in the United States. For example, Lall and Siddharthan (1982) believed that because U.S. firms dominate most domestic industries, the intangible assets of entire foreign industries would be unlikely to be great enough to generate patterns of foreign investment in the United States. Kim and Lyn (1987) pointed out that research and advertising intensity by U.S. companies creates barriers to the entry of new foreign firms, thereby discouraging foreign investment. Several studies, however, have uncovered an apparent relationship between advertising and/or research expenditures and foreign investment in the United States (Kahley, 1987; Franko, 1976; Kim and Lyn, 1987; Little, 1984). In their study, Kim and Lyn reported contradictory findings in the case of advertising.

The literature indicates that simply the presence of firm–specific advantages does not alone explain FDI. In order to explain why firms choose to exploit these advantages through direct investment, authors such as Dunning (1980) and Rugman (1981) have turned away from a concentration on industry–wide behavior to theories pertaining to the growth and behavior of the individual firm. They have noted that intangible assets such as marketing skills could presumably be exploited in an export operation without a direct investment abroad, and have stressed that some additional motivation must be present for a firm to choose the route of foreign production. Cost differences, trade barriers, and the need to be near customers can provide this motivation and contribute to the foreign investment decision. Furthermore, in analyzing why companies choose to exploit intangible assets through production operations abroad rather than through product licensing arrangements, researchers have shown that manufacturing abroad is often preferred because negotiating a fair price for intangible assets is difficult or because of a fear of losing control over proprietary knowledge (Rugman, 1981; Caves, 1971; Markusen, 1984).

The importance of markets as an attraction for foreign manufacturing operations is a common thread running through theories of FDI. For example, while theories based on the characteristics of oligopolies focus on industrial structure as an explanatory factor, they recognize, at least implicitly, that the advantages of product differentiation and intangible assets are unlikely to lead to foreign investments unless attractive markets are present as well.

This emphasis on market factors has been supported by evidence from statistical studies and surveys of foreign investors in both the United States and other countries. In a study of 39 foreign companies that made new investments in the United States between 1974 and 1978, the size of the U.S. market was the single most important reason cited for the investments (Ajami and Ricks, 1981). Similar results were found by Morrow (1975), Davidson (1980), and Kahley (1987). Scaperlanda and Maurer (1969), the U.S. Department of Commerce (1973), Green and Cunningham (1975), Davidson (1980), and Ajami and BarNiv (1984) all found a relationship between some aggregate measure of market size, such as Gross National Product, and levels of foreign investment or growth rates in foreign investment.

In summary, recent theoretical and empirical work has led to the general conclusion that four principal factors must be present to induce a firm to undertake foreign investment: (1) firm–specific advantages that will enable the firm to compete successfully with local companies, (2) a preference for local manufacturing over exporting, (3) a desire to exploit assets through ownership of local manufacturing facilities rather than licensing, and (4) attractive markets. These conditions are based on the assumption that products manufactured overseas are primarily for consumption in the countries where they are produced. When products are manufactured abroad for export markets, the conditions may be different. In that case, access to raw materials or inexpensive labor may be prime considerations.

Recent theoretical and empirical work indicates that any given firm is likely to cite a number of reasons for its decision to invest overseas. The reasons include desires to exploit technological advantages, to achieve cost benefits, to gain access to raw materials, to take advantage of favorable currency exchange rates, to reduce transportation costs, to overcome trade barriers, to avoid difficulties of licensing agreements, and to respond to the actions of competitors. Each of these factors is discussed in Part 3 of this publication.

Little of the research discussed in this section is based on field studies or interviews; the studies depended on mail surveys or searches of the literature, including government publications and corporate data. One notable exception is Aharoni's careful review of the foreign investment process of U.S. firms. The author describes the "initiating forces" that lead managers in U.S. companies to focus attention on the possibility of investing abroad. One such initiating force is a strong interest by one or more high-ranking executive in the company. Another force is a proposal or suggestion from a foreign distributor, client, or other outsider. Fear of losing an export market because of import restrictions, getting on the "bandwagon" with other successful investors, and retaliating against strong competition from abroad are other forces. With some likelihood that an attractive opportunity may exist, according to Aharoni, the next step is an investigation that will serve as a basis for the decision. A comprehensive investigative checklist is suggested consisting of political, economic, market, production, operating cost, capital requirement, plant–location, and other factors. After those investigations, risk and uncertainty are evaluated. The decision to invest may be conditional on final negotiations abroad. A period of negotiation with foreign nationals then ensues, in which the details are finalized.

PLANT-LOCATION THEORY AND RESEARCH

One conclusion emerges clearly from past research regarding the plant–location decision process: firms typically approach the location decision as a multistage process (Tong, 1979; Schmenner, 1982; Blair and Premus, 1987). In most cases, companies first choose a region, and only then do they begin to evaluate specific communities and sites. Wardrep (1985) found that over half the companies he surveyed first chose a region or group of states before beginning detailed analysis of sites (Blair and Premus, 1987). A survey of 204 firms in the Southeast found that most firms chose the Southeast first and then looked at specific sites (Hekman, 1982). Consequently, most of the sites that were considered but not chosen were also in southeastern states.

The factors considered during the two stages can vary considerably. In the first stage, a few high priority items are used to identify those states that satisfy the most important criteria. Schmenner identified these items as the company's "must list." Important considerations at this point are the availability and cost of labor and proximity to markets (Blair and Premus, 1987). For example, Schmenner found that for many companies concerned about unions, the first step is to look only at right–to–work states.

Schmenner, Huber, and Cook (1987) pointed out that all the states passing the first cut generally will be rated highly and differ only slightly on the factors considered the most important screening criteria. These factors are thus no longer the most important at the next or second stage of evaluation. Site–specific factors such as land costs, access to roads, and quality of schools then become important (Schmenner, 1982; Blair and Premus, 1987).

Most companies eventually narrow their search to three or four communities (Hack, 1984). By that stage, the remaining communities will be almost equal on cost factors and it will be other, noncost factors that will tip the scales in favor of one community or another. Schmenner terms these desirable factors, which can be traded off against one another, the firm's "want list."

One final observation regards the importance of mathematical and computer methods of analysis in plant–location decisions. Clearly, firms are equipped today with the tools to conduct rigorous analyses of costs and benefits of potential sites. With the exception of some large, multiplant firms, however, most surveys found that few companies are using these sophisticated tools (Stafford, 1980; Blair and Premus, 1987). Instead, they make something of an educated guess regarding location of their plants. Also, ironically, just at the time when the tools for rigorous location analysis are improving, research indicates that nonquantifiable, subjective factors are assuming more and more importance in the plant–location decision process.

The literature contains a great deal of information on the location factors taken into account by firms when making site selection decisions. Plant–location theory has grown substantially in scope and complexity in the period since Alfred Weber described the process in 1929 as a problem of minimizing transportation costs (Blair and Premus, 1987). Weber and others believed that the optimal location would minimize the total combined cost of transporting raw materials to the plant and finished products to the market.

Later theorists recognized that other costs, such as energy and labor, needed to be taken into account as well. Realizing that no single location would minimize each individual cost, they viewed the optimal location as the one that would minimize total costs — trading higher costs on one item for even lower costs on another. Renner (1947) suggested that cost minimization could be achieved by locating near the production factor that would be most difficult to transport, such as raw materials, skilled labor, or power. Clearly, this factor would differ among industries and individual companies (Tong, 1979).

In the 1950s, theorists began to expand their view of plant-location decisionmaking to include noncost factors. For example, Greenhut was the first to emphasize the importance of being close to potential markets (Tong, 1979). Stafford (1980) further stressed the importance of proximity to markets as a means of achieving better customer communication and service.

In developing his thesis, Greenhut also pointed out that a firm interested in maximizing its profits would search not just for a site with the lowest costs, but for a location that would maximize the difference between revenues and costs. Isard and Goldstein recognized that profit maximization might not be the only objective and suggested that personal preferences of managers might also be involved in the decision (Blair and Premus, 1987). Since that suggestion was made, researchers have placed greater emphasis on noneconomic factors, such as a location's quality of life and the advantages of being located near firms in the same industry. As transportation has improved, firms are apparently making plant–location decisions more on the basis of factors other than transportation costs for raw materials or finished products (Schmenner, 1982).

Numerous studies have assessed the relative importance of various site location factors. Most were based on surveys, but some have used econometric analyses of the relationship between patterns of actual plant locations and the location factors used in selecting them. These studies have yielded a wide variety of results. For example, transportation was cited as a key factor in studies by Hekman, *Inc.* magazine, *Industry Week*, the Joint Economic Committee, and Kieschnick (Blair and Premus, 1987). Labor availability was found to be a significant factor by *Inc.*, Kieschnick, *Fortune*, and the Joint Economic Committee. Labor costs were cited only by Kieschnick and the Joint Economic Committee.

Access to markets is another factor frequently identified as having a major impact on plant–location decisions (*Inc.*, Kieschnick, *Fortune*, and the Joint Economic Committee). Taxes were found to be important by *Fortune*, *Industry Week*, the Joint Economic Committee, and Stafford. Other factors mentioned less frequently include the cost of land (Hekman, 1982), proximity to universities (Joint Economic Committee), availability of capital (Kieschnick), access to raw materials (Kieschnick), unionization (*Industry Week*), business climate (Hekman), and labor productivity (Hekman).

One of the most comprehensive studies of site selection decisions was Schmenner's survey of *Fortune 500* companies in 1982. He found that proximity to markets and labor considerations such as wage rates and levels of unionization were easily the most important factors for these companies. Other important considerations included proximity to suppliers, nearness to other company facilities, and quality of life.

In an approach that distinguished his research from others, Schmenner tried to identify the location priorities of 11 specific industry groups based on characteristics such as capital and labor intensity, use of perishable inputs, and market orientation. Not surprisingly, the priorities of these groups varied widely. For example, industries that served broad geographical markets with commodity type products like lumber and basic chemicals were likely to cite transportation costs as a primary concern. On the other hand, labor–intensive, import–threatened industries like shoes and apparel placed more emphasis on labor costs. High–technology industries, being less constrained by labor and transportation costs, attached greater importance to such factors as quality of life when evaluating potential sites.

A few studies have dealt specifically with the location decisions of foreign firms or have compared the behavior of foreign–owned companies with that of domestic companies. Like research on location decisions by U.S. firms, these studies have yielded widely varying results.

For example, Tong (1979) surveyed 242 foreign–owned manufacturing firms and found that the most important factors affecting their location decisions were transportation services, labor attitudes, space for expansion, nearness to markets, and availability of a site. The least important considerations were cost and availability of capital, nearness to home country, proximity to export markets, and nearness to operations in third countries.

In a survey of 21 West German and Japanese firms located in the Charlotte/ Mecklenburg, North Carolina area, Chernotsky (1983) found that availability of desirable sites, attractiveness to incoming personnel, and market access were the most important considerations. Less emphasis was placed by these firms on labor, financial incentives, and access to raw materials and semifinished goods.

A study by Little determined that foreign investors placed more emphasis on wage differences and the availability of ports than did U.S. firms, while U.S. companies were more concerned about fuel costs. On other factors, there was little difference between the two groups (Kahley, 1986). Like Little, Kahley also compared location decisions of U.S. and foreign firms, and he found no significant differences.

Few generalizations can be made about the relative importance of various site selection factors. They appear to differ in influence depending on the industry, the raw materials used, the skills needed, the type and area of market, company size, previous experience with labor unions, personal preferences, and other factors. Finally, for any given firm, the various decision factors receive different attention at different stages of the decision process, such as selection of a geographic region (described below).

In addition, the priority accorded to individual location factors may change over time. For example, during periods of rapidly rising petroleum prices, concern with transportation costs may be strong on the part of many firms. In a time of labor shortages, availability of labor may be an overriding concern, at least for some industries and regions. Overall, Blair and Premus have noted that proximity to raw materials appears to have become less important, while proximity to markets has gained in influence. Generally, they believe that traditional factors such as labor, nearness to markets, and transportation costs are still the most important, but they are becoming less dominant, and noneconomic factors such as quality of life are receiving more attention than in the past.

RESEARCH METHODOLOGY

Our research methodology differs in three important respects from the more typical approaches for previous studies, described above. First, our research is based principally on field interviews with executives of 20 U.S. affiliates or subsidiaries of foreign companies. In all but a few cases, the executives cooperating in the field research had played a key role in the site selection process they were describing. This field research was supplemented by an intensive literature search.

Our heavy reliance upon open–ended inquiry during the interviews was a second major difference in our approach. During the interviews, we did not ask the executives to rate predetermined location factors, such as nearness to markets or favorable wage rates. Rather, our questions were nondirective and broad:

Why did your company build manufacturing facilities in this country?

How did you go about making your plant-location decision?

What were the principal factors that influenced your site selection decision?

In contrast to the more conventional process of ranking predetermined location factors, we believe the open–ended inquiry singles out and highlights the most important factors in the decision process while minimizing the attention given to a host of less important considerations. In our opinion, the respondents tended to focus on the principal advantages of one location relative to another — the differences that weighed heavily in the final decision. In concentrating on such differentiating factors, however, the executives sometimes ignored considerations that were of roughly equal significance in two or more locations.

During the interviews, a total of nineteen different location factors were identified by executives in the twenty companies. As a final check for accuracy and completeness, we sent each participating executive the complete list of nineteen factors, marking the specific factors they had identified as being "very important" or "moderately important" during the interviews. With a list of nineteen factors before them, eight of the participating executives re–thought their response, expanding the number of location factors they considered significant.

Our inquiry into various facets of the management process involved in site selection is a third significant difference between our approach and that of most others.

Who was involved in the analysis and decision?

In what order or sequence were the analyses and decisions made?

Fourth, in our interviews with executives in the foreign companies, we attempted to determine the extent to which original expectations about operations in the United States had been met. We asked three open–ended questions regarding the experiences to date:

Relative to your expectations when you made the decision to locate here, how have things worked out?

Have you encountered any problems you did not anticipate?

Have you experienced any pleasant surprises?

The field work was conducted with executives of foreign companies that had established manufacturing operations in Virginia in recent years. Executives in 22 companies were asked to participate in the study, and 20 agreed. Interviews were held in the plants or offices of 15 companies; telephone interviews were completed with the five remaining companies. The timing of the plant start–ups is shown in Table 1.1.

Table 1.1

PLANT START-UP TIMING

START-UP DATES	NUMBER OF PLANTS
Prior to 1981	1
1981 — 1985	3
1986 — June, 1988	13
Announced (Not yet operating in July, 1988)	3
TOTAL	20

We focused on recent plant start–ups to increase the likelihood that persons intimately involved in the decision would still be accessible for interviews. Managers' recollections about the decision would be vivid because the events were recent. Concentrating on the experiences of the past few years would also provide the greatest insights into contemporary location decisions.

We also interviewed officials employed by economic development agencies in both Virginia and North Carolina. Virginia was selected because the 20 plants were located in the state. North Carolina was picked for two reasons: In many cases, North Carolina is competitive site–wise with Virginia, and North Carolina has an excellent economic development reputation. Economic development officials in both states were asked questions such as:

How does your agency promote foreign direct investment in your state or community?

How is contact with foreign clients established and maintained?

How do state and local economic development agencies interact in working with foreign clients?

The corporate managers and the economic development officials are identified in Table P.1 of the preface.

The findings of our research are reported in Parts 1 through 4 and in an appendix.

Part 2 examines Management Strategies. Investment Strategies — the market, cost, and other strategies that drove the investment decisions in the 20 foreign companies — are described. It also covers Operating Strategies that guided manufacturing operations after the plants were built, and it reviews some of the recent Operating Experiences of the Companies.

Part 3 specifically covers the Plant-Location Decisions. The integral managerial aspects in the decision making process are analyzed in the section entitled Managerial Process. The section entitled Location Factors by Company sets forth the location factors considered important by executives of the companies in the survey. Observations on Key Location Factors — their character and signficance — are also set forth in this part.

Part 4, entitled Individual Company Characteristics and Decisions, provides a Profile of the U.S. Company for each of the 20 foreign affiliates in the survey, setting forth product and other information about each. The management process followed in each company in making its location decision is depicted in a Decision Sequence.

Our conclusions and additional data on current FDI trends are presented in Part 5 and in the appendix.

Part 5, the Summary and Conclusions, reviews the research findings and offers our thoughts about them. The findings are compared with the work of earlier researchers, and the implications for business executives, economic development professionals, politicians, and state and local administrators are given.

The appendix presents salient Foreign Direct Investment Trends. Data on the number of foreign affiliates, the amount of direct investment, and employment are provided for selected years beginning in 1977. The analysis covers the United States, the Southeast Atlantic region, and the state of Virginia — the region and state in which the 20 plants studied here were ultimately located.

PART 2

MANAGEMENT STRATEGIES

This part is concerned with key managerial strategies. As we visited with managers of the foreign companies, we discovered that a number of market, cost, and other strategies guided the decisions to invest in the United States, and these fundamental strategies continued to be important after the plants had commenced operations. Personnel, technology, organizational, and other strategies also continue to influence day–to–day operations in the post–start–up period.

Executives were explicit in describing some of the strategies; others could be inferred from comments, actions, and observations during the visits. We have also included some of our impressions about the effectiveness of the strategies.

INVESTMENT STRATEGIES

The key strategies guiding the decisions to establish manufacturing operations in the United States are shown in Table 2.1. The decisions were heavily market–driven in 14 of the companies. In four additional companies, cost and market strategies were of about equal importance. Thus, marketing strategies were important in 18 of the decisions. Key marketing rationales included the attractiveness of the U.S. market, the desire to improve customer service, and the need for additional capacity to meet market demands.

The investment decisions were predominantly cost–driven in two companies. In four companies, as noted, marketing and cost strategies shared prominence. Thus, cost strategies were significant in six of the decisions. Compelling cost considerations included the desire to reduce total costs, the effort to reduce transportation costs relative to those for exported products, and the transitory existence of favorable foreign currency exchange rates.

As noted in Table 2.1, the potential for improving customer service was highlighted in eight of the interviews. The prospect of reducing transportation costs was specifically mentioned by executives in seven companies, including some in which marketing considerations were of paramount importance. Seven executives also commented on the effects of changes in the foreign currency exchange rates and how those changes had influenced their decision, at least the timing of the action. The ability to avoid tariffs by local manufacture was cited in three interviews. In the following paragraphs, the major marketing and cost strategies are explored.

Table 2.1

KEY STRATEGIES DRIVING THE INVESTMENT DECISIONS

TYPES OF STRATEGIES	NUMBER OF DECISIONS
MARKET STRATEGIES (such as *Participate in Attractive U.S. Market, Improve Customer Service,* and *Provide Capacity to Meet Market Demands*) **WERE THE PRIMARY DRIVING FORCES IN THE DECISIONS**	14
COST STRATEGIES (such as *Reduce Total Costs, Reduce Transportation Costs, Benefit by Favorable Fluctuations in Foreign Currency Exchange Rates,* and *Avoidance of Tariffs*) **WERE THE PRINCIPAL DRIVING FORCES IN THE DECISIONS**	2
MARKET AND COST STRATEGIES WERE OF ABOUT EQUAL IMPORTANCE IN THE DECISIONS	4
TOTAL DECISIONS	20

SELECTED STRATEGIES	NUMBER OF TIMES MENTIONED
IMPROVE CUSTOMER SERVICE	8
BENEFIT BY FAVORABLE FLUCTUATIONS IN FOREIGN CURRENCY EXCHANGE RATES	7
REDUCE TRANSPORTATION COSTS	7
AVOIDANCE OF TARIFFS	3

Participate in the U.S. Market

The attraction of the U.S. market was a key consideration in every case, and local manufacture was viewed as a way of strengthening competitiveness in the market-place. An executive of one company summed up the feeling in almost every organization with these words,

> *The U.S. market for our product is the largest and most attractive in the world. We have to be in it with as much strength as possible.*

Improve Customer Service

A manufacturing presence in the United States was seen as a strategy for strengthening ties with old customers and cultivating new ones. One executive remarked,

> *Much in business is done informally. It's hard to do business here from an office in Europe.*

Reflecting the thinking of executives in 12 different companies, one said,

> *We wanted to be as close to the customers as possible. It was the main thing.*

Using similar words, another observed,

> *Being near to our customers, we can cut down on manufacturing and delivery lead times. We see our customers more often, so it's easier to iron out problems. Being close should help us expand our market share.*

Still another executive commented this way on the importance of marketing in the location decision:

> *We were not happy with our manufacturing reps. Instead of going halfway, continuing to export and using our own U.S. sales force, we decided this was the time to go all the way — manufacturing here and selling with our own people.*

With respect to channels of distribution, most of the companies seemed to move through comparable stages of using distributors or brokers for their initial penetration of the U.S. market, followed in time by the establishment of sales offices with in–house personnel.

Implement Product Strategies

With regard to product strategies, some executives reasoned that a U.S. base would help in the process of designing or tailoring products to the needs of their U.S.

customers. Interestingly, with regard to product positioning, our impression was that the products offered by 19 of the 20 companies were designed and produced for the premium, high–priced end of the various markets in which they were sold.

Attain Advertising and Promotion Objectives

In most companies, the initiation of manufacturing in the United States was accompanied by a shift in responsibility for advertising and promotional activities from the parent company to the U.S. affiliate. One executive commented,

We can do a much better job working with ad agencies and sensing customer reactions by directing advertising from here.

Why the decision to shift the responsibility for the advertising function was made at the same time as the manufacturing decision is not exactly clear. We suspect that a local manufacturing operation provides a management structure here that encourages or permits still other functions to be handled locally.

Maintain Customer Service by International Expansion

Three of the twenty companies we interviewed decided to initiate manufacturing operations here after a principal customer of each made the move to the United States. The three companies had been supplying parts and components to customers in their home country, and they wanted to continue the relationships in the United States. One commented,

We felt we could meet the needs of our customer better with U.S. manufacturing than we could with exported materials.

All three companies designed their plants, however, with capacity well above that needed to supply the prime customer who prompted the investment decision. The excess capacity will be used to cultivate a diversity of new customers throughout the country. As one executive observed,

We had been thinking about the possibilities of manufacturing here. When [our customer] made the move, we thought it was a good time for us, too. It gives us a good start-up volume for our plant.

In effect, each of the three companies followed a strategy of using one large customer whom they followed from abroad to provide the base load for their own plant here. It provided the economic wherewithal for them to develop the entire U.S.

market from a local plant.

Enhance Cost Competitiveness

Objectives involving cost competitiveness were dominant in less than one–third of the decisions, but they played some part in almost every case. The companies pursued strategies to reduce costs and control expenses. One executive said,

The total delivered costs for our products are lower from our new U.S. plant than they are from our plant in [the parent country]. Savings in freight offset any manufacturing disadvantages we have here.

Another commented,

Labor costs aren't too bad here. In [the home country] we have more costs for guaranteed employment, insurance, health, and other employee benefits. Overall, labor may be less expensive here.

Hedge Foreign Currency Exchange Fluctuations

Most executives appeared to view their U.S. operations as a hedge against unfavorable fluctuations in foreign currency exchange rates. The inevitable fluctuations in exchange rates would sometimes favor a manufacturing location here, sometimes one abroad. Because the managers were aware of the volatility in monetary exchange rates, they did not see the less expensive dollar in 1988 as a long–term advantage. Summing up the posture of several managers, one said,

The exchange rate situation influenced the timing of our decision, but we had long–term strategic reasons for being here.

We would expect a protracted continuation of existing foreign exchange rates (favorable to investment in the United States) to have a salutary effect on the pace of FDI here. In start–up situations, the lead time from a decision to manufacture in this country to the time of plant start–up tends to be long, often two to five years. The investments now being examined are relatively less expensive to the Japanese, West Germans, and British than those being evaluated three years ago, when the dollar was more expensive.

With regard to company acquisitions, the right timing for a deal, from a foreign currency exchange standpoint, could mean everything in terms of the quality of the investment. Initial investments tend to be higher for acquisitions than for plant start–ups because of the premium paid for going–concern values. As a consequence, the cost of an acquisition to a foreign company is highly dependent on the exchange rate at any moment.

Develop a Global Strategy

Executives in several companies viewed their U.S. manufacturing decisions, in addition to market and cost strategies, as integral parts of their global strategies in which major worldwide markets would be served by local manufacturing plants. One executive commented,

> *A manufacturing facility in the United States will help us achieve a corporate goal of becoming a global corporation.*

Five of the twenty companies in the study indicated that they had a global strategy, including manufacturing in countries other than their home countries and the United States. For them, the addition of a manufacturing facility in the United States was not their first venture abroad. The decision to operate here was made to solidify their positions in the U.S. market, then being served by exports.

Achieve Profitability and Return–On–Investment Objectives

During our interviews with executives, direct references to profitability and return–on–investment occurred infrequently. Passing comments were made, however, about corporate and divisional objectives for profitability and return–on–investment as market and cost strategies were being explained.

OPERATING STRATEGIES

We observed and discussed various facets of ongoing company operations during our on–site visits. Certain operating strategies were stated explicitly during these conversations. In addition, our observations of the manufacturing operations and comments by executives about them allowed inferences about other strategies (described in the following paragraphs). We do not repeat here market strategies, such as customer service, or cost strategies, although they are, of course, just as applicable to ongoing operations as they are to the investment decision.

Technology and Plant Equipment

These companies are relying extensively on state-of-the-art but proven technology. Computer–controlled processing equipment was in evidence in at least ten of the plants. The process equipment was modern and impressive, as one would expect of new manufacturing operations. The machinery and equipment was also preponderantly of foreign manufacture, often duplicating or upgrading the equipment being used in the foreign plants of the parents. Summing up the opinions of a number of executives, one stated,

> *This equipment is the best we can buy. It is as good or better than the equipment we are using at home.*

One company has a sophisticated management control system using computer and telecommunications technologies. It has an on–line computer connection between its Virginia facility and its headquarters abroad for a variety of accounting, financial, manufacturing, and inventory systems.

Except for one leading–edge manufacturing process, which we agreed not to discuss, we do not believe there is much in the way of experimental or less than fully–proven technology being used.

Almost all of the plants were carefully laid out to facilitate the flow of inventories from the raw material or component stage through processing or assembly to finished goods warehousing. The assembly lines were automated, and extensive use was made of various types of materials–handling equipment, including overhead cranes, mechanized conveyor belts, gravity conveyors, forklift trucks, and a computerized automatic warehousing operation, where boxes and inventory are picked from storage and moved to a loading platform by computer-controlled robotic technology.

Decentralized Management Philosophy

Each of the U.S. managers has been delegated a great deal of authority by superiors in the foreign company. The local managers have broad discretion on a wide range of policy and operating matters — pricing, recruiting, and procurement. In most cases, complete freedom has been granted on wage and salary levels as well, although approvals from abroad are required in some companies for actions involving higher paid personnel. One executive sized up the situation this way,

> *In our company, we feel we have more local autonomy than is customary in companies from [our home country]. We have the authority to do just about anything we need to do.*

In every company, manufacturing operations were conducted within the framework of well–developed operating plans or budgets. The operating plans (sales and manufacturing expenses) were developed by the managers of the U.S. plants and agreed upon with executives of the parent companies. As actual results are obtained, the managers of the U.S. affiliates explain departures from anticipated sales expenses or budget levels.

Every company is subject to fairly rigid capital expenditure constraints. These costs are budgeted, and specific approvals are required from the parent companies for all but nominal amounts. Summarizing the process, one manager said,

> *They come over to visit once a year. We need approval to spend capital. Outside of that, we just have to explain when we miss the budget.*

In our judgment, the degree of management discretion and autonomy given the U.S. executives in these foreign companies is significant and allows local managers to be flexible and responsive to changes in local conditions.

Managerial and Technical Personnel Policies

In view of the policy of many highly successful multinational corporations to employ local nationals to lead their foreign operation, we were somewhat surprised by the number of U.S. operations headed by nationals from the home countries. Foreigners led 17 of the 20 companies we visited, filling roles such as chief executive officer, chief operating officer, president, or plant manager. In all 17 cases, the nationality of the resident general manager was that of the owning company. Almost every manager of a U.S. operation was an employee of the parent on temporary assignment in the United States.

U.S. nationals, however, filled most of the management positions below the level of general manager. The number of foreign personnel in general management positions seldom exceeded two, although there were four foreigners in one company and five in another.

The number of technical people on temporary assignment to U.S. operations ranged up to four, except for one company that had 35 foreign nationals in technical assignments. Many of the foreign technical personnel are in the United States on three–year job assignments. Commenting on technical support personnel, one manager remarked:

> *We need trained technical people from [our home country], but we can't offer a salary that is attractive. The salaries of our people get out of line with those of U.S. workers, and the budget won't permit it anyhow.*

The U.S. immigration laws limit the number of foreign nationals in key managerial and technical slots. The regulations with respect to work permits and visas make it difficult to use foreign nationals in cases where Americans with substantially the same personal qualifications are available for specific jobs. The total number of foreign nationals in the companies is relatively low, as noted, but we could not tell whether the immigration laws or management preferences were the more important causes.

Our impression was that most of the executives, naturally, wanted to present their company in a positive light. Nevertheless, although they were not anxious to discuss problems or possible errors in judgment, a number of interesting and revealing comments were made about their U.S. experience, which are reported under the heading *Operating Experiences of the Companies*.

Export Strategies

Each of the companies intended initially to concentrate on the U.S. market, with some exports to other North American countries such as Canada and Mexico. One manager summed up the viewpoint:

For the time being, our hands will be full with the U.S. market.

Many of the companies did, however, view their new U.S. facilities as potential sourcing points for overseas exports at some time in the future.

Executives in two companies saw their U.S. operations also as potential supply points for their home market at some future date. In one of these companies, the total delivered costs of U.S. products in the home country were expected to be below those of products produced abroad. The principal cost advantages of the U.S. location were expected to be lower raw material costs and, taking into account the burdens of employee benefits and work guarantees overseas, lower labor costs.

During our interviews, few other executives spelled out future exporting plans in any detail and there was no reference to specific business plans for exporting. Perhaps such plans exist but were simply not shared with us.

Compensation Policies

Every operating manager outlined a policy of paying fully competitive wages and salaries for employees. One commented,

We were attracted to this area by the prevailing wage rates, and we don't want to be responsible for bidding them up, but we do want to be completely competitive.

The managers seemed to be particularly sensitive about their responsibilities in being competitive with employee benefit programs. One remarked,

The practices here are different from those in [our home country]. We are relying upon employee benefit consultants to make sure we are doing what

we should.

In one company's industry, wage levels are commonly at or near the minimum wage rate. The company followed these prevailing practices. The firm was experiencing profit difficulties, and the management felt severe constraints in administering its wage and salary program. Conditions were particularly difficult because there were a number of higher paying industries in the area.

Several companies expressed concern about possible salary "bidding wars" for skilled technical personnel. Many had found it necessary to train personnel needing special skills, and there was a marked uneasiness about possible salary escalation for these employees, particularly if there was another company in the same area using the same job skills.

Corporate Image

All the executives showed some concern about how their company — with its foreign ownership — would be perceived in the United States by customers, employees, and the public generally. We observed a strong and deliberate commitment on the part of every manager to have the foreign affiliates recognized as "good corporate citizens" in their adopted country. As a consequence, there was an obvious readiness to participate in community affairs such as the United Way.

We also observed a deep concern about employee safety and an appreciation of environmental issues. Some managers observed that the local regulations on air, water, and waste were less restrictive than those to which they were bound in Europe and Japan.

Procurement

Although they have made the transition to a U.S. manufacturing base, most of the companies still relied heavily on their own facilities or suppliers abroad for purchases. Large numbers of components or parts were being brought into the United States for assembly or further processing. Several of the managers voiced sensitivity about the amount of non-American purchases.

As a matter of future policy, most of the managers announced their intention to make substantial and increasing use of U.S. sources and suppliers. Interestingly, several companies pointed to a common intermediate–term goal, summed up by one executive as follows:

As an objective, we plan to purchase at least 50 percent of our requirements from U.S. suppliers.

For some companies, local natural resources and agriculture play an important part in the raw material picture. One company relies on a nearby soapstone deposit and quarry. Another has established a vineyard in the state. A third uses large local supplies of wood, and a fourth depends on nearby livestock and meat–processing plants.

Union Attitude.

There was a diversity of opinion about unions but, as noted previously, many of the companies established operations in Virginia because of their desire to avoid areas having strong union sentiments. One manager summed up his feelings this way,

It is a psychological thing. We are accustomed to unions at home and believe we know how to deal with them. Maybe we'll get one here in time. Until then, things are simpler without a union.

Another executive stated,

We have had a union in [another state] for many years, and, frankly, we just don't want to deal with it anymore.

Two managers made substantially similar remarks that tied together concepts of fair employee treatment and concerns about unionization. One observed,

We are trying very hard to treat our employees fairly, so there will be no need or desire on their part to unionize.

OPERATING EXPERIENCES OF THE COMPANIES

During the interviews, the executives of the foreign affiliates were questioned about their experience operating their plants in the United States. (The specific questions asked are listed in the background section, which discusses our research methodology.) In particular, as noted, we inquired how things were proceeding relative to original expectations. The responses to our questions fell into five broad categories related to labor and personnel, management performance, operations, product, and quality–of–life issues.

The unanticipated problems mentioned most frequently pertain to labor and personnel. For example, the foreign companies experienced significant problems in complying with immigration regulations. Six executives spoke of "inordinate delays, hassles, petty harassment, and overt roadblocks" caused by the Immigration and Naturalization Service (INS). Employee visa problems were so serious for one company that it decided to leave critically needed engineers at home rather than face the INS obstructions that threatened their entry into the United States. One foreign executive summed up the feelings of many of his fellows by stating,

> *I don't understand it. Your country courts us and welcomes our investment. We're given incentives to locate here. Then the INS treats us like criminals every time we try to enter the country. It's really rather insulting.*

Executives in three companies were disappointed with the overall quality and productivity of their work forces, citing lack of motivation and poor work habits. Three others had concerns about employee skill levels and training; executives had to provide much more in-house training than was originally planned. Several European executives attributed low skill levels to the absence of formal apprenticeship training in U.S. vocational programs.

Another unanticipated problem was difficulty convincing foreign nationals to relocate to this country. In one case, the problem was compounded by budget constraints that prevented management from offering wages high enough to induce relocation.

In spite of immigration and other problems, not all experiences with labor and personnel matters were negative. Two executives repeatedly mentioned how delighted they were with the quality and productivity of their workers. Several executives cited high loyalty, low turnover, and excellent labor availability as very positive factors. (Other labor issues are discussed in Part 3 under the heading *Labor Supply, Skills, and Work Ethic*.)

Several parent companies encountered unanticipated problems with the original management team responsible for their U.S. subsidiaries. In one case, the problem was so severe that the owners contemplated a complete shutdown of the U.S. operation after five years of losses. Instead, the manager of the U.S. operation was replaced, and the company's owners were surprised by how quickly the situation improved under new leadership. Sales more than quadrupled in the next four years, with a corresponding increase in profits.

In another company, the manufacturing layout designed by the original management of the U.S. subsidiary proved to be very inefficient. The present general manager informed us that the entire plant layout would have to be redesigned in order to bring operating efficiency up to acceptable levels.

At another company, an interpreter was present at an interview to assist with a foreign chief executive officer who did not speak fluent English. This manager alluded to communication problems that had delayed the plant's construction and start–up phases. We do not know how much effect, if any, language difficulties had on this problem.

Another company experienced a costly setback because it relied on a foreign project manager who was not familiar with U.S. construction practices. Based on plans originally developed abroad, this manager supervised the construction of a building with walls below the thickness requirements of U.S. insurance companies.

The renovation required to bring the facility up to insurance specifications caused a 20 percent overrun on total building costs.

The intricacies of U.S. tax laws caused a problem for at least one of the foreign–based companies. Interest and penalties resulted from nondeliberate tax underpayments on tax returns that were prepared in the home country.

Several executives commented on air, water, and waste controls, as well as construction codes. No problems in understanding or compliance were reported, however, and several executives noted that regulations tended to be less restrictive in the United States than they were abroad.

A problem cited by one executive resulted from making and selling an industrial product component that the executive believed was "too good for the U.S. market." The product specifications, determined by designers in the home country, were significantly above those required by the U.S. market. Thus, marketing problems were encountered in trying to convince customers that the product was worth a premium price. Problems with this product were exacerbated by difficulties in training workers to meet the demanding specifications.

Another company also encountered problems in introducing a high–quality, premium product to consumer markets. The company was experimenting with sales and advertising methods, but sales to date had been significantly below target. In the opinion of the executive we interviewed, the wholesale distribution system in the United States was the crux of the problem. He found the system "formal, cumbersome, and unresponsive to dealer needs." Interestingly, a nonpremium product of this company was doing far better than expected, setting sales records month after month. In the original planning abroad, this product had been projected to be only moderately important.

The problems cited here must be placed in the context of an overall success enjoyed by these companies. Most of the executives indicated that their operations were proceeding either satisfactorily or extremely well relative to original expectations.

SUMMARY

Strategic objectives relating to marketing effectiveness and cost competitiveness led the companies in our study to make their U.S. plant investment decisions. Previously, the firms had been serving the U.S. market by exports from their home countries, but difficulties were perceived with this arrangement, most importantly customer service problems stemming from distance. Also, operating and transportation costs were sometimes higher than they might have been with local manufacturing capability. Thus, distinct profitability incentives existed. Psychologically, moreover, the companies were anxious to make the type of long–term commitment to the U.S. market that is represented by a major manufacturing plant investment.

While all companies shared a common desire to be as cost–competitive as possible, attaining exceptionally low operating costs did not appear to be a realistic corporate goal. Not one executive mentioned a corporate strategy based on low unit manufacturing costs. Such a goal may not have been attainable. Although the plants are modern, with what appear to be excellent labor efficiencies, they are comparatively small relative to the largest establishments in their industries. An indication of plant size is given in Table 2.2, which shows the number of plants by size of employment. Seventeen of the plants have fewer than 100 employees. In such small plants, indirect costs (for supervision, insurance, depreciation, and other related expenses) tend to be much higher per unit of output than in larger establishments, and it would be difficult for these plants to be the most cost–effective in their industries.

Six of the new plants were operating well below designed capacity levels in 1988. Market reasons explained the below–capacity operating levels in some situations,

Table 2.2

EMPLOYMENT IN PARTICIPATING COMPANIES

NUMBER OF EMPLOYEES	NUMBER OF PLANTS
0 – 49	8
50 – 99	6
100 – 249	4
250 – 499	1
500 and over	1
TOTAL	20

while start–up production problems existed in others. We estimated the operating levels at 35 to 60 percent of capacity in these six plants. Revenues in these operations were probably not sufficient to cover all the fixed costs of depreciation and overhead. The managers did not, however, seem unduly preoccupied with short–term profitability performance. One stated,

> *We have long-term strategic reasons for being in the United States, and we built a plant large enough to meet our market needs in several years.*

Useful conclusions about the technological and operational strategies of the companies can be inferred from our research. The plants are modern, using the very latest in technology. They have excellent materials-handling equipment, and they appear to be labor–efficient. Sophisticated computer–controlled processing equipment benefits operations in at least half of the companies. In terms of management philosophy, decentralized management concepts prevail, with considerable local autonomy delegated to local managers.

The companies are determined to blend effectively into the U.S. culture and business environment. A deep interest in the well–being of employees, a social consciousness, and "buy American" policies are testimony to this determination. On the other hand, the predominance of foreign general managers is a clear reminder that the companies are owned and controlled by non–U.S. interests.

PART 3

PLANT-LOCATION DECISIONS

This part of the book describes the processes followed by foreign companies to select plant locations in the United States. The first section covers the managerial processes, and the second section identifies the specific location factors considered important by executives in the study. The third section discusses each of the location factors in some detail.

MANAGERIAL PROCESS

Our research included an inquiry into a major aspect of management's role in making foreign direct investments — the process involved in making plant–location decisions. Based on this experience, we are able to present some general conclusions about the character of the process that we believe have significance for anyone interested in attracting foreign manufacturing investment to a locality.

The decision to establish a manufacturing plant in the United States is ordinarily made by the board of directors or by the principals of the foreign company. Initially, the decision to manufacture abroad is a conditional one, subject to the development of a specific investment recommendation which covers a particular site, building, and investment costs. After the conditional judgment is made, several actions are ordinarily taken: (1) a project manager is designated to find a suitable U.S. site, (2) certain broad criteria (to be discussed) are established to guide the search for a location, (3) a specific site is found, and (4) the definitive costs for items such as land, building, machinery and equipment, and inventory are determined.

In some rare cases, the decision to invest in the United States and the decision to operate in a specific plant were made almost simultaneously. These situations arose when a highly unusual business opportunity involving a specific plant site was presented to a management as a package.

In most companies, the site selection process involved three fairly distinct stages: the selection of a specific geographic region in the United States, the selection of states within that region, and the final decision on a specific site in a particular community. As will be noted, however, the number of stages varied from one to four in the companies we studied.

Because of the economic development emphasis of our work, we considered only new plant start–ups, not acquisitions of established manufacturing operations. Start–ups, including the purchase of buildings but not of ongoing operations, were selected because they often create a greater economic impact than acquisitions of U.S. companies, at least initially. A plant start–up results in new jobs and fresh investments in plant and equipment. An acquisition involves a change in company ownership of a plant, but the number of jobs and nature of the facilities may stay much the same.

The managerial process described below is applicable to most situations we encountered, but there are exceptions. In two companies in our study, for example, the firms already had manufacturing plants in the United States at the time new Virginia plants were opened. In those instances, the managerial process for locating a new facility was different from the process used in locating a company's first U.S. plant. One principal difference related to the strategic positioning of the new plant relative to the location of the existing facilities. Moreover, if product options existed, a company had to decide which products to manufacture in the new rather than the established plants.

Selection of Specific Geographic Regions

As the first stage in the site selection process, managements of foreign companies usually select one or more regions of the United States that are attractive to them. Fifteen companies in the study began their site search in this manner. Because of unusual circumstances, the other five companies bypassed the regional– and state–selection stages entirely and focused immediately on a specific site or area in Virginia. In these special cases, the approaches were dictated by the location of a vineyard, a quarry, a large customer, or joint venture partners.

Of the 15 companies, seven concentrated their search in one region (the Southeast), five restricted their search to two regions, and three companies considered as many as three or four regions. The other regions under evaluation were the West Coast, the Middle Atlantic, and the Midwest.

Our conversations with executives revealed that the site selection studies they conducted were not particularly rigorous, at least when compared with certain comprehensive approaches suggested in the current topical literature. In most cases, land, construction, taxes, labor, and other operating costs were not collected and compared for various regions of the United States. More commonly, a presumption from the outset was that one region (the Southeast, for example) was the least expensive, or the most attractive. The Japanese companies did appear, however, to be particularly methodical in their approach.

Of course, the suppositions about a region were not based purely on caprice — our research indicates that executives of foreign companies usually had fairly strong regional insights gained prior to the time of the site selection process. Apparently, a body of knowledge is shared informally by foreign executives about the strengths and weaknesses of different geographical regions of the United States. This sharing occurs in private conversations, at social gatherings, at conferences, and in other settings where executives "network." These impressions may be modified by executives' personal travels in this country, by media exposure, or by business experiences. In short, regional, state, and community reputations are made and lost by networking and other informal exposures that create strong positive and negative predispositions before the executives begin the formal site selection process.

Most of the executives we visited seemed to have certain common perceptions about the Southeast that existed before the executives viewed specific sites and tended to be sustained during the site selection process. Specifically, the region is perceived to embody certain strengths. Portions of the Southeast are located strategically for serving the major metropolitan areas of the Northeast and even the Midwest. The region is seen as having excellent seaports, including Baltimore, Maryland; Norfolk (Hampton Roads), Virginia; Wilmington, North Carolina; Charleston, South Carolina; and Savannah, Georgia. The Southeast is also viewed as having a moderate cost of living, with reasonable wages and other expenses. It has a reputation for harmonious labor relations and for employees with a good work ethic. Finally, there is a belief that the region has favorable quality–of–life attributes, including a desirable climate and good recreational opportunities. This particular bundle of perceived benefits attracts many companies to the Southeast, just as other benefits are effective in drawing companies to the Midwest, the West, the Southwest, or other areas.

There are negative perceptions about the Southeast as well. The lack of adequate numbers of skilled or highly trained manufacturing employees is one. Concern about general levels of education is another. Despite the Research Triangle in North Carolina and the area around Atlanta, Georgia, the region is not seen as having as much of a research and development orientation as some other regions. Lack of financial sophistication because of remoteness from major financial centers bothers some. Finally, some executives see problems with air transportation schedules and facilities, and with a highway system that is not good in all areas of each state, particularly in remote areas.

In summary, the process for selecting a particular region is not necessarily based on rigorous analytical work or on careful comparisons. We heard few references to detailed comparisons of wage rates, utility rates, tax rates, or other cost factors. The regional decisions are more than intuitive — being based on prior knowledge, impressions, or preconceptions — but they do not appear to reflect intensive study of all possible options.

Selection of States

Selection of one or more states within a region is usually the second stage in the site selection process. Our research reveals less about why foreign companies home in on specific states within a region than about why they select a particular region in the first place. About half of the fifteen companies that went through the regional– and state–selection process narrowed their choices to two or three states prior to the evaluation of specific sites. No company restricted its search to just one state. Three companies — one beginning with six states, one with five states, and one with three — narrowed their choices to two states before beginning intensive site–selection work. Another company narrowed the number of states from four to one before doing site work. Still another company considered every state in the Southeast fairly carefully. Thus, no clear–cut pattern emerges, but there was a predisposition to concentrate the hunt for sites in just two or three states.

All of the plant–location factors that apply in evaluating a region are, of course, important in contemplating one or more states within a region, but the companies exhibited more specificity in their thinking about states than about a region. For example, one or two states in a region may be located more advantageously with respect to a desired seaport. Airline service from one point may be superior to service from another. Differences in labor availability exist. Thus, even with the use of broad criteria for selection, choices are made within a region.

Other phenomena are at work as well, however. The perceived vitality of a state is a critically important element in the decision to consider it as a potential location. A positive and receptive attitude is generated by factors such as abnormally high indicators of economic growth, unusual success in attracting new manufacturing plants, a high population growth rate, and other positive factors. The reputation of some states is enhanced by the activities of the economic development officials located abroad. Officials in these offices play an important role in familiarizing the foreign business community with the characteristics of their states. Participation by state officials in trade shows abroad also contributes to this process. Trade missions conducted by governors and their staff members are highly visible efforts to acquaint foreign executives with the advantages of specific states. A number of states budget substantial sums to advertise their merits in foreign periodicals.

Selection of a Specific Site in a Particular Community

The search for a specific site ordinarily begins after a company has chosen two or three likely states. Most companies contact state economic development agencies for assistance at this juncture. The agencies respond by drawing up lists of specific sites and buildings for the foreign clients to examine, based on specific criteria provided by the companies. In addition to many of the criteria described previously for selecting regions or states, the site-specific criteria also include requirements for acreage, building size and layout, interstate highway accessibility, railroad siding availability, utility specifications, desirable community characteristics, and so on. Sites meeting these criteria are identified by state economic development officials who draw upon computer data bases, suggestions from regional and local economic development officials, and their own knowledge of sites across the state.

The state economic development agency in Virginia ordinarily draws up a list of four to six sites for each client. In North Carolina, on the other hand, the number of sites suggested is often somewhat greater, ranging between four and 12 locations.

After they have compiled the list of prospective locations, Virginia economic development representatives arrange a site and community tour for the foreign executives. The tours are sometimes made in a state–owned airplane. On other occasions, a state vehicle is used. At each location, the visiting delegation is joined by local economic development officials and frequently by members of the business community. These trips often require two to three days.

As soon as the executives of a foreign company show enthusiasm for a specific site, the economic development officials from that area assume the prime responsibility for interactions with the foreign executives, taking over from the state officials. Negotiations regarding zoning, support from the local community, building design, utilities, access roads, and other matters are resolved at a local level. In North Carolina, state officials retain general control of the process, even when specific local sites are being assessed.

The managerial process regarding site selection ends when a tentative location is chosen and the decision is reported back to the home office for final review and ratification. The critical evaluation of a site in relation to the established criteria ends the process.

It should be noted that the final decision to locate in a specific state, such as Virginia, is not ordinarily determined until the final decision on a site is made. Most companies consider sites in two or more states in the final selection process. When one of those sites is selected, the state in which the company will operate is selected *ipso facto*.

LOCATION FACTORS BY COMPANY

This section presents our findings with regard to the specific factors that determined these companies' site–selection decisions. Table 3.1 is a matrix in which the significant location factors are arrayed by company. The 20 companies across the top of the matrix were all interviewed by us. Nineteen of the companies are identified by name. One company requested anonymity. Detailed information on the companies in the study is given in Part 4.

Factors important to the companies in making the location decision are shown along the side of the matrix. Under each company name, dots have been placed to indicate the important location factors mentioned to us by executives in that company. The factors marked with a black dot were identified by the executives as being "very important" in conditioning their decisions. The factors marked with a shaded dot designate considerations that were "moderately important."

The location factors shown on the matrix were developed in a two–step process. As the first step, location factors were identified by executives in each company during personal interviews. The location factors were given in response to an open–ended question:

What were the most important factors that led you to select this location for your plant?

The executives were asked to indicate the degree of importance — either "very important" or "moderately important." In the interviews, we did not suggest specific factors, nor did we provide a list of location factors for the respondents to rate. The nineteen different location factors shown in the matrix, such as nearness to markets, were cited by one or more executives as being either "very important" or "moderately important."

As the second step in our study of location factors, executives were asked by mail to confirm or to modify the specific reasons they had mentioned previously during the personal interviews. Each executive was sent a matrix similar to the one in Table 3.1, except that each matrix showed dots only for the reasons specified by that company. Each executive was asked to validate the information or to alter it, if desired. With nineteen location factors to consider, including the ones they had originally identified, eight of the executives elected to make some changes in their ratings.

Table 3.2 summarizes the company responses provided during the interviews and in the follow–up process. The table shows the number of companies mentioning each factor during each of the two steps. The total number of factors rated as "very important" by the 20 companies grew from 65 to 70. The number of factors deemed "moderately important" by the 20 companies increased from 40 to 58. Thus, the total number of important location factors mentioned by companies grew by 23. As noted above, these changes were accounted for by executives in just eight of the 20 companies, and two companies accounted for over half of the entire increase.

The overall importance or ranking of individual location factors was not changed materially by the second step in the rating process. Except for wage rates, mentioned by five companies on follow–up as compared with one during the personal interviews, there were no other significant changes. Nine of the 19 location factors were mentioned by two more companies on follow–up, two factors were mentioned by one more company, one factor was cited by one less company, and there were no changes at all for six of the 19 factors.

In discussing an important factor during the interviews, such as the availability

Table 3.1

LOCATION FACTORS BY COMPANY

Legend: ● = primary factor ◎ = secondary factor

Company	LOGISTICS — Nearness to Markets	Proximity to Raw Material Sources	TRANSPORTATION — Seaport Accessibility	Air, Rail, and Highway Transport	LABOR — Labor Supply, Skills, and Work Ethic	Wage Rates	Right-to-Work Laws	FINANCIAL — Land, Building, and Tax Costs	Economic Incentives
WEIDMULLER	●		◎	◎		◎	◎	◎	◎
WALTER GRINDERS			◎	◎					
VSL CORPORATION							●	◎	●
VDO-YAZAKI	●		●						
UNIDENTIFIED	●		●	◎			●	◎	◎
SUMITOMO	●		●				●		
SAN-J	●		●	◎	◎		●		
OPTON	●			◎			●	◎	◎
NEW ALBERENE	●		●		●	●	●	●	●
LINGUANOTO		●						◎	◎
INTERTAPE	●	◎	●		●	●	●	●	
HERMLE				◎	●		●		◎
G.D PACKAGE	●						●		
FRANZ HAAS	●							◎	
FIORUCCI	●		●				●	◎	
ERNI	●	●					◎		◎
D-SCAN									
CANON VIRGINIA		●	◎	◎	●	◎	●		◎
BARBOURSVILLE	◎		●	●	●	◎	●	◎	
ALLIED COLLOIDS		◎	●		◎		◎		

34

Table 3.1 (continued)

Legend: ● Very Important Factor ◉ Moderately Important Factor

	ECONOMIC DEVELOPMENT AGENCIES	QUALITY OF LIFE	BUSINESS CLIMATE	NEARNESS TO HOME COUNTRY	SPECIAL CLIMATIC CONDITIONS	PROXIMITY TO COMPETITORS	JOINT VENTURES	VIRGINIA HISTORY AND CULTURE	POSITIONING OF ADDITIONAL PLANTS	DISTANCE FROM RESIDENTIAL HOUSING
INTANGIBLES				**OTHER**						
WEIDMULLER			◉	●						
WALTER GRINDERS		●	●							
VSL CORPORATION						●				
VDO-YAZAKI	◉				●					
UNIDENTIFIED	●	◉	◉							
SUMITOMO	◉	◉								
SAN-J		◉				●		●	●	
OPTON	◉	◉	◉							
NEW ALBERENE										
LINGUANOTO				●						
INTERTAPE	●			●					●	
HERMLE	◉									
G.D PACKAGE										
FRANZ HAAS		◉	◉							
FIORUCCI	●	◉	◉	●	●					
ERNI							●			
D-SCAN	◉	◉					●			
CANON VIRGINIA	◉	◉							●	
BARBOURSVILLE		●		●					●	
ALLIED COLLOIDS	●	●		●						●

35

Table 3.2

NUMBER OF COMPANIES MENTIONING VARIOUS LOCATION FACTORS AS BEING VERY IMPORTANT OR MODERATELY IMPORTANT

	DURING INTERVIEWS			AFTER REVIEW		
	VERY IMPORTANT	MODERATELY IMPORTANT	TOTAL	VERY IMPORTANT	MODERATELY IMPORTANT	TOTAL
LOGISTICS						
NEARNESS TO MARKETS	12	0	12	12	1	13
PROXIMITY TO RAW MATERIAL SOURCES	3	2	5	3	2	5
TRANSPORTATION						
SEAPORT ACCESSIBILITY	8	1	9	9	2	11
AIR, RAIL, AND HIGHWAY TRANSPORT	1	5	6	1	7	8
LABOR						
LABOR SUPPLY, SKILLS, AND WORK ETHIC	2	3	5	5	2	7
WAGE RATES	1	0	1	2	3	5
RIGHT-TO-WORK LAWS	9	3	12	9	5	14

Table 3.2 (continued)

FINANCIAL						
LAND, BUILDING, AND TAX COSTS	2	6	8	2	8	10
ECONOMIC INCENTIVES	1	7	8	2	8	10
INTANGIBLES						
ECONOMIC DEVELOPMENT AGENCIES	6	6	12	5	7	12
QUALITY OF LIFE	3	5	8	3	7	10
BUSINESS CLIMATE	0	2	2	0	4	4
OTHER						
NEARNESS TO HOME COUNTRY	4	0	4	5	0	5
SPECIAL CLIMATIC CONDITIONS	4	0	4	4	2	6
PROXIMITY TO COMPETITORS	2	0	2	1	0	1
JOINT VENTURES	2	0	2	2	0	2
VIRGINIA HISTORY AND CULTURE	2	0	2	2	0	2
POSITIONING OF ADDITIONAL PLANTS	2	0	2	2	0	2
DISTANCE FROM RESIDENTIAL HOUSING	1	0	1	1	0	1
TOTAL	65	40	105	70	58	128

37

of transportation facilities, executives did not usually indicate the stage of the location decision to which the answer applied — the selection of a geographic region, the choice of one or more specific states, the selection of a particular locality, or the decision to acquire a specific property. In the first few interviews, we asked the respondents to associate their reasons with specific stages in the decision process:

What were the important factors leading you to select the Southeast region, what considerations were important in picking Virginia, and what factors led to a final plant location?

This stage–by–stage approach was not particularly effective, however. Certain key reasons for the plant–location decisions seemed to stand out in the managers' reflections about the decision process, and these reasons were not easily identifiable with one stage or another.

The matrix has a dot for every important reason mentioned by the executives, except for a few site–specific factors that were mentioned infrequently, such as the amount of land, building size, and plant layout. Some site–specific considerations such as railroad (siding) availability and land, tax, and utility costs, are included, however.

Many of the final sites under consideration were located in industrial parks with infrastructures of roads, utilities, water, waste disposal, and railroad sidings already in place. Competing sites were often of roughly equal attractiveness in such key respects. Also, many of the buildings were constructed to specifications after a location had been selected, so competing building attributes was not usually a factor.

In explaining their site decisions during the interviews, the executives tended to focus on those factors that differentiated one site from another. They were less likely to mention a site factor if a competing location appeared to have somewhat the same advantage, even if the factor was relatively important. That is, factors of about equal attractiveness tended to "wash" in the decision process.

A discussion of one factor — wage rates — may be helpful in explaining how the rating process, with its emphasis on differentiating characteristics, can be interpreted. As indicated on the matrix, out of 20 companies only two considered wage rates a "very important" location factor and three considered them a "moderately important" factor, despite the comparatively attractive levels of wages in Virginia and the rest of the Southeast (see later discussion). Interestingly, as noted above, during the interviews only one executive cited wage rates as being "very important" and no executive cited wage rates as "moderately important." Perhaps these ratings are explained by the fact that almost all of the final competing sites were in the Southeast, where wage rates tend to be generally lower than in some other regions. Thus, wage rates was not a differentiating or decisive factor in the final judgment on sites within the region.

This reasoning does not explain, however, why wages were not considered an important regional location advantage. Since wage rates in the Southeast are generally lower than those in the Midwest and the Northeast (and this regional advantage was obviously well known to the executives in the study), this phenomenon is surprising. Perhaps other employment factors such as labor availability and right–to–work laws were considered so important that they displaced wages as an important consideration.

A brief summary of the findings set forth in the matrix follows:

Nearness to markets, right–to–work laws, the role of economic development agencies, and seaport accessibility are the factors that were considered "very" or "moderately important" by the greatest number of companies.

The role of economic development agencies was viewed as being either "very important" or "moderately" so by most of the executives.

Economic incentives; quality of life; and land, building, and tax costs were considered important factors in half of the 20 decisions.

Air, rail, and highway transport and labor supply, skills, and work ethic were important factors in somewhat less than one–half of the cases.

Nearness to home country — an East Coast location for European or Canadian parent companies — was significant in one–fourth of the decisions.

Unusual factors, mentioned only once or a few times, could nevertheless be very important to the particular company involved. A satisfactory climate for manufacturing (temperature, humidity, or air salinity) was important in some cases. A plant location remote from established housing was important to a chemical company. Proximity to competitors was important to one company for market visibility and other reasons, including the availability of a skilled labor pool.

Utility costs, often covered in site selection literature, are not even shown on the matrix; no executive mentioned this factor. Perhaps utility costs are a significant but nondifferentiating type of factor.

Another location factor discussed frequently in site selection literature is also missing on the matrix. Nearness or easy access to colleges, universities, or research centers was not mentioned by anyone. The absence of this factor may be explained by the fact that these foreign–owned operations are not involved in much, if any, research and development work in this country; that is being done by the parent companies abroad.

The number of important factors identified by executives is not particularly large, which implies that the managers were discerning in their answers. The number of "very important" factors in each decision ranged from one to five. The number of "moderately important" considerations also ranged from one to five. Overall, the number ranged from one to nine.

In the paragraphs that follow, each of the location considerations set forth in the matrix is discussed in detail.

OBSERVATIONS ON KEY LOCATION FACTORS

In the following analysis of plant–location factors , we have three objectives:

1. to define the plant–location terminology,
2. to examine the thinking of the executives about these factors,
3. to provide some background about each factor so that the thinking of each executive can be put in some perspective.

Nearness to Markets

Writers in both scholarly and popular journals have focused on the need to be close to customers in order to gain a competitive edge in the business environment. The desire to have a manufacturing base close to their U.S. markets and customers was significant in 13 of the 20 plant–location decisions. It was "very important" for 12 companies and "moderately important" for one.

Foreign firms face inherent disadvantages in terms of nearness — language and culture barriers, ocean and distance barriers, tariff and customs barriers. Long shipping distances require long lead times. Foreign managers, design engineers, and marketing experts are less able than their domestic counterparts to follow the rapid changes in domestic consumer tastes and industrial product requirements. For these reasons, customer service sometimes suffers when companies export to the United States from foreign manufacturing points.

All but one of the companies in the study exported to the United States prior to the time facilities were constructed in Virginia. The exception, a food company, was barred from exporting to the United States by a U.S. Department of Agriculture ban on all Italian meat imports. Local production was the company's only option if it wanted to exploit the huge food market in America. The other 19 companies found advantages in American manufacture that justified considerable investment.

As noted earlier, after the decision to establish manufacturing operations in the United States has been made, the desire to be close to customers continues to play a dominant role in the selection of a particular region and state. Virginia was attractive to the foreign managers because of its position near the heavily populated and industrialized northeastern states. Virginia also combined this locational advantage with other favorable factors common to the Southeast, such as the price of land, the level of taxation, and labor relations. Indeed, Virginia's unique position as the most northerly of the southern states makes it a favored location for many manufacturing firms wishing to service both southern and northern customers.

For example, a tractor–trailer originating in Richmond can travel as far as Massachusetts or Florida in one day. If a circle with a radius of 600 miles is drawn with its center in Richmond, the encompassed area includes 50 percent of the national population, 52 percent of U.S.–manufactured durable goods sales, and 48 percent of total retail sales. In addition, it encompasses over half of Canadian wholesale and retail sales. Thus the executives viewed a location in Virginia as beneficial to their marketing efforts throughout much of North America.

A special example of staying "close to the customer" may occur when large foreign companies establish manufacturing operations in the United States, because generally such manufacturers have many suppliers of parts and components in their home countries. These suppliers sometimes build their own U.S. facilities near the plants of the major manufacturers in order to provide better customer service, to deliver products more quickly, and to benefit from cost advantages. Lower costs can include reduced transportation expenses, lower wages (in some cases), and the absence of tariffs. In addition, suppliers benefit by demonstrating loyalty and commitment to their major customers, thus helping to foster a favorable business relationship.

A well–documented instance of this phenomenon occurred when Nissan Motor Corporation built its first American automobile plant in Smyrna, Tennessee. Since the plant's opening in 1981, many Nissan suppliers have constructed new plants in Tennessee and neighboring states to supply the facility. Several of these suppliers have used Nissan as an initial key customer, then developed other U.S. customers.

In our study, two companies built facilities in Virginia to supply foreign customers who had established operations in the United States. One company opened a facility in northern Virginia specifically to supply instruments and gauges to the Volkswagen plant in Westmoreland County, Pennsylvania. This company has since expanded its customer base to include the major American automakers as well as customers in other industries. Another company was a longtime supplier to Canon in Japan. This company decided to open a plant in Virginia after Canon opened its Newport News facility. Although the supplying company still relies on Canon for 80 percent of its business, it hopes eventually to generate 60 percent of its U.S. sales from other customers.

Proximity to Raw Material Sources

Five of the 20 companies were attracted to locations because they were close to sources of raw materials. For three of the companies, this was "very important," and for two it was "moderately important." For a manufacturer of soapstone stoves, the need for a supply of soapstone with the proper heat–retaining properties pointed the company's management immediately to Virginia because the state has the only acceptable vein of soapstone in the Western Hemisphere. A meat–processing company wanted a location close to suppliers of quality fresh beef and pork. A location south of Richmond placed the company near cattle and hog growers in southern Virginia and northern North Carolina. In the case of a furniture manufacturer, the factory needed to be close to particleboard suppliers. This condition was met by a location in the South Boston area, which has many lumber mills nearby.

The other 15 companies did not mention proximity to raw material suppliers as a major factor in choosing a location. In at least one of these cases, in fact, the Virginia location was actually a disadvantage. This manufacturer ships electronic components from Asia to Seattle, Washington, where the parts are transferred to trucks for transport to Virginia. The fact that Virginia was selected for the plant site rather than Seattle or some intermediate location indicates that factors other than material availability were more important for this particular company.

An important adjunct to the issue of locating near raw material sources is the prevalence of the use of imported materials by the companies in the study. Many import a significant percentage of their raw materials, components, and subassemblies from home facilities and from other countries. A furnituremaker brings in teak veneer from Southeast Asia and hardware (screws, connectors, and other findings) from Europe. A manufacturer of photocopying equipment imports components and subassemblies from many different countries, including its home country, Japan. These parts are assembled into finished units, and some of the finished units are exported to Japan. A maker of cigarette and candy packaging machines imports all its machinery components from Italy. It assembles the machines either at its Richmond facility or directly at the customer's site.

Companies are importing components for U.S. assembly rather than importing finished products for three principal reasons. First, tariffs are often lower on components than on finished goods. Second, labor rates are currently lower in the United States than in some other countries. Third, certain products can be shipped more inexpensively unassembled than as finished products. One example is furniture, which is bulky and expensive to ship once assembled.

The managers of several importing companies had stated goals of increasing the percentage of domestic raw materials and components they used to at least 50 percent of all purchases. The following reasons were given for this policy: to minimize the price volatility of imported materials caused by fluctuating exchange rates, to avoid duties and tariffs, and to benefit from improved delivery schedules and shorter lead times. As noted previously, decisions to increase purchases from U.S. suppliers also have political overtones. Foreign executives are sensitive about their roles as non–Americans with plant ownership in this country and take a number of steps to put an American imprint on their operations. One such step is the increased procurement of American components, assemblies, and other parts for manufacture.

Seaport Accessibility

Executives in nine of the 20 companies sought ready access to a quality deepwater seaport. Nine considered this criterion "very important" and two considered it "moderately important." To five of these companies, a location within 100 miles of a deepwater port was absolutely essential. Access to a major seaport was mentioned more frequently than requirements involving other modes of transportation — air (commercial and passenger), rail, and highway. Nearness to a seaport with excellent harbor facilities was also important to a number of companies' export plans for finished products.

Frequently, a location near a seaport kept overall transportation costs low by minimizing the distance and the transfer time from dockside to factory. It also allowed immediate response when complications arose during loading and unloading operations or while goods were clearing customs. The executives preferred plant locations near either Hampton Roads, Virginia (the Tidewater area) or Baltimore, Maryland. When alternate locations were mentioned, they were generally near other southeast Atlantic seaports such as Wilmington, North Carolina; Charleston, South Carolina; and Savannah, Georgia.

Air, Rail, and Highway Transport

Executives in eight companies mentioned availability and quality of air, rail, or highway transportation as significant location factors. These factors were considered "moderately important" in seven companies and "very important" in one. Some executives who had not considered transportation issues significant at the time locations were chosen felt differently after the plants became operational.

The need for good air transport facilities and convenient schedules was emphasized by executives in several companies, particularly those that relied on air delivery to bring in lightweight electronic components or to ship rush orders to customers. Quality service was also stressed by a manufacturer of large machines who used air transportation to import machinery parts for assembly.

One executive noted, however, that the development of overnight air-delivery services afforded his company great flexibility in deciding where to locate a U.S. facility. According to this executive, manufacturers of electronic parts have the freedom to locate in any U.S. community where overnight delivery service is available.

Passenger airline travel is another important facet of the transportation picture.

Airlines are used by company employees to travel to their home countries, to other international destinations, and to other U.S. points. One executive favored a site in northern Virginia because of its location near the Washington, D.C. international airports. In general, the executives spent considerable time flying to and from their home countries and their customer locations, and they were extremely conscious of differences in the quality of air service between various states and various airlines.

With the exception of Dulles Airport near Washington, D.C., passenger service in Virginia received fair or poor ratings from the executives. They were disappointed by the limited number of direct flights to major U.S. cities and the lack of direct flights to foreign cities — factors that caused time–consuming layovers in intermediate cities. Managers mentioned Richmond and Norfolk specifically as cities lacking good air connections. To these managers, the decision to locate in Virginia was made in spite of the problems they associated with air service there.

North Carolina economic development officials explained how similar problems had hampered their efforts, especially in the period before direct international flights were initiated from the Charlotte and Raleigh airports. We were told of one large foreign manufacturer who chose Georgia over North Carolina because the Atlanta airport offered advantages. The North Carolina officials were hopeful that expansion in the number of direct flights from Charlotte and Raleigh to international destinations would benefit the state in the competition for foreign manufacturing investments.

Because our interviews were limited to executives of companies in Virginia, the study excludes companies that chose other states because of the lack of international flights from Virginia airports. We surmise, however, that companies have located in other states to take advantage of superior international air connections.

Judgments about rail and highway transportation seemed to have more relevance to decisions about specific sites than they did to decisions about regions or states. States in the Southeast all have well-developed highway and railroad systems. We do not know of any southeastern states that were eliminated from consideration during the site selection process because of poor railroads or highways. The consideration of specific sites, however, was very dependent on the quality or condition of rail and highway access. For example, several companies required railroad spurs on their properties and eliminated any sites lacking them. Another company, whose products move both north and west by truck, rejected many sites before a site near the intersection of two major interstate highways was found.

For the reasons just cited, communities with an interest in economic development are very conscious of the importance of rail and highway transportation. Their promotions and presentations emphasize any competitive advantages they may enjoy in this regard.

Labor Supply, Skills, and Work Ethic

Executives in seven of the 20 companies mentioned the importance of an available labor pool, along with the skills and attitudes of employees in it. This factor was cited as being "very important" in five companies and "moderately important" in two. These executives were interested in communities where there was an adequate pool of unskilled laborers as well as a reservoir of workers with certain technical and trade skills. They were also interested in communities where employees had positive attitudes and possessed a generally good "work ethic."

Assessing the availability of labor in an area is difficult. One yardstick is the level of unemployment within a state. Typically, low unemployment is indicative of a tight labor market. Using this yardstick, Virginia, with its extremely low unemployment rate, would certainly appear to be one of the least attractive of the southeastern states. Unemployment rates for the United States as a whole and for states in the Southeast are shown in Table 3.3. Note that most states in the Southeast had unemployment levels in 1988 below the level in the United States as a whole.

Table 3.3

UNEMPLOYMENT FIGURES
UNITED STATES AND SOUTHEASTERN STATES

APRIL, 1988

SOUTHEASTERN STATES	NUMBER UNEMPLOYED (thousands)	PERCENT UNEMPLOYED
DELAWARE	11.1	3.2%
DISTRICT OF COLUMBIA	17.2	5.2
FLORIDA	304.0	5.0
GEORGIA	179.6	5.8
KENTUCKY	145.9	8.6
MARYLAND	95.8	4.0
NORTH CAROLINA	109.4	3.4
SOUTH CAROLINA	74.0	4.5
TENNESSEE	125.2	5.3
VIRGINIA	105.9	3.5
WEST VIRGINIA	71.5	9.7
UNITED STATES	6,359.0	5.3%

Source: United States Department of Labor, Bureau of Labor Statistics, *Employment and Earnings, May & June, 1988.*

Despite low levels of unemployment, a number of companies in the study were spectacularly successful in recruiting workers. Some reported large numbers of applications for jobs; one company received 22,000 applications for just 550 jobs.

These were cases of attractive companies with sound compensation policies moving into tight labor areas, and the corporate moves drew positive media publicity.

Two executives mentioned specific important location strategies involving the availability of employees. The president of one company outlined the strategy of being a significant employer, though not necessarily the largest, in a small town. He believed this strategy was an excellent one for attracting employees. Another executive wanted a location in an area that was largely rural, because this strategy would reduce the likelihood that employees would "job hop" after they had been trained.

Subsequent to the location decisions, not all companies were pleased with the labor availability in their chosen areas. In a number of situations, the decision to locate in the United States was made when domestic unemployment was high, but the labor market later tightened up. One CEO remarked,

When we came here, there was a good supply of unskilled labor. With the pickup in economic activity and other new plants, unemployment has fallen from 11.1 percent to 7.9 percent, and things are getting a little tight.

Managers of several European companies commented on the continuing problems they were experiencing in attracting adequate numbers of suitably skilled employees — problems that did not exist in their home countries. This problem has exposed the companies to unexpectedly high training costs. One European manager was distressed about employees he had sent to the home plant for training. Two resigned almost immediately upon their return to the United States to accept higher paid jobs with other companies. Nearly all of the managers found it necessary to provide technical training to bring employees up to satisfactory skill levels. Some of this training was unanticipated.

The importance of employees' work ethic was mentioned frequently in the interviews. Several executives were attracted by Virginia's reputation for having workers who are conscientious and hardworking. Two executives said that the actual work ethic was even better than they had expected.

Accolades for Virginia workers were not universal, however. One executive was very disappointed with the work habits and the lack of commitment among his employees. In another case, although we were told by the plant manager that the employment situation was satisfactory, the executive's U.S. subordinate painted a different picture, expressing doubts about employee motivation. He was having difficulty hiring enough workers who met his standards, despite a high rate of unemployment in the region.

Wage Rates

Wage rates were considered a significant location factor in five companies. The factor was rated "very important" in two cases and "moderately important" in three. One CEO stated,

We chose Virginia because labor rates were 30 percent less than in the Northeast.

There was a widespread belief among the executives that wage rates in Virginia were very competitive. Data in Table 3.4 compare the average weekly earnings of production workers on manufacturing payrolls in Virginia and in other selected states for April, 1988. Virginia's weekly earnings and average wage rates are generally in line with those of other states in the Southeast and below those of states in the Northeast and Midwest.

Our study indicates that it is this regional difference that attracts investors, not the attractive wage rates of any one state in the region. We believe other companies did not single out wages because the differences in wages among various southeastern states and communities in them were not perceived as being large. One executive made this point by stating,

Wage rates are so comparable that they are not too much of a factor.

We do not know why more executives did not emphasize wages as a critical factor in the regional decision process, however.

Right-To-Work Laws

State right–to–work laws prohibit union shops. Where unqualified union shop agreements exist, an employer must require union membership as a condition of employment for all nonsupervisory plant employees. At the time of employment or shortly thereafter, an employee must join the bargaining unit and continue as a member in good standing. Otherwise, the employee will be discharged.

The Taft–Hartley Act of 1947 modified the forced–membership feature of the union shop. Changes were made because union shop agreements were believed to infringe on the rights of people who had strong religious or personal convictions against union membership. Under the provisions of the act, employees need not actually join and be active in the union of a shop, provided they pay union initiation fees and dues.

Section 14(b) of the Taft–Hartley Act subjected the union shop provisions of collective bargaining agreements to state law. The act gave individual states the authority to pass "right–to–work" legislation, which makes even the forced payment of dues illegal. Thus, the term "right–to–work" is somewhat misleading. The legislation does not guarantee the right to work; it protects workers from dismissal if they do not wish to pay union dues.

Virginia, which passed a right–to–work law in 1947, is one of 20 states with such legislation. The right–to–work states and the years in which the legislation was enacted are shown in Table 3.5. The list is heavily populated with states in the Southeast, South, Southwest, and the Plains. Regions such as the Middle Atlantic, New England, and the West Coast have little representation.

Table 3.4

AVERAGE WEEKLY EARNINGS OF PRODUCTION WORKERS ON MANUFACTURING PAYROLLS
SELECTED STATES, APRIL, 1988

	WEEKLY EARNINGS	PERCENT ABOVE (BELOW) VIRGINIA
VIRGINIA	$ 389.16	0.0%
OTHER SOUTHEASTERN STATES		
DELAWARE	$ 422.01	8.4%
DISTRICT OF COLUMBIA	440.61	13.2
FLORIDA	334.95	(13.9)
GEORGIA	355.56	(8.6)
KENTUCKY	406.42	4.4
MARYLAND	423.10	8.7
NORTH CAROLINA	326.03	(16.2)
SOUTH CAROLINA	342.38	(12.0)
TENNESSEE	370.35	(4.8)
WEST VIRGINIA	446.76	14.8
OTHER STATES		
ILLINOIS	$ 461.62	18.6%
MASSACHUSETTS	420.02	7.9
MICHIGAN	581.56	49.4
NEW JERSEY	444.96	14.3
TEXAS	416.07	6.9

Source: United States Department of Labor, Bureau of Labor Statistics, *Employment and Earnings, June, 1988.*

Much research has been carried out to ascertain the effect of right–to–work laws on the levels of unionization within individual states. Table 3.6 compares the levels of unionization in selected right–to–work states with the average level in non–right–to–work states and in the total U.S. nonagricultural labor force. The data in this table suggest a negative correlation between right–to–work laws and levels of unionization. Unionization in the right–to–work states, all in the South and Southeast, is well below that in the non–right–to–work states and in the United States as a whole. It should not be assumed, however, that the right–to–work laws are the cause of these low levels of unionization. It is possible that unfavorable public attitudes toward unions lead to both low levels of unionization and to the passage of right–to–work laws, and that unions were already weak in right–to–work states before the legislation was enacted.

Table 3.5

RIGHT-TO-WORK STATES
SHOWING YEARS LEGISLATION WAS ENACTED

LEGISLATION ENACTED		LEGISLATION ENACTED	
DURING THE 1940s	**YEAR**	**DURING THE 1950s**	**YEAR**
Arizona	1946	Alabama	1953
Arkansas	1947	Mississippi	1954
Florida	1944	Nevada	1951
Georgia	1947	South Carolina	1954
Iowa	1947	Utah	1955
Nebraska	1946	**DURING THE 1960s**	
North Carolina	1947	Wyoming	1963
North Dakota	1947		
South Dakota	1946	**DURING THE 1970s**	
Tennessee	1947	Louisiana	1976
Texas	1947	**DURING THE 1980s**	
Virginia	1947	Idaho	1985

Sources: Keith Lumsden and Craig Petersen. "The Effects of Right-to-Work Laws on Unionization in the United States." *Journal of Political Economy* 83 (December 1975); p. 1242; and U.S. Department of Commerce, Bureau of the Census. *National Data Book and Guide to Sources: Statistical Abstract of the United States*, 1988.

An early study by Lumsden and Peterson (1975) reviewed existing statistical studies and considered impressions of employers, employees, and unions. They said that the existence of right–to–work laws is negatively correlated with levels of unionization. However, they conclude that the low levels of unionization in right–to–work states are the result of attitudes toward unions rather than of the right–to–work laws themselves:

> *Our general conclusion, therefore, with regard to states which have adopted right–to–work laws is that they hold significantly different attitudes regarding unionization than do the remainder of the states, but that no evidence*

exists of any significant impact on unionization of the actual right–to–work laws themselves.

Thomas Carroll (1983) refutes this conclusion, however. He attempts to account for public attitudes toward unions by analyzing variables such as levels of education and labor force diversity. His research finds that state differences on these measures do not explain the low levels of unionization in right–to–work states. Therefore, he concludes that right–to–work laws do have an impact on levels of unionization. He also finds that right–to–work states have lower wage rates on average, which he believes is an indication of the power of right–to–work laws to weaken unions' collective bargaining strength.

Table 3.6

LEVELS OF UNIONIZATION IN SELECTED STATES NONAGRICULTURAL WORK FORCE

1982

SELECTED RIGHT-TO-WORK STATES IN THE SOUTHEAST AND SOUTH	PERCENT OF WORK FORCE UNIONIZED	RANK AMONG STATES
SOUTH CAROLINA	5.8%	51
NORTH CAROLINA	8.9	50
MISSISSIPPI	9.3	49
FLORIDA	9.6	48
VIRGINIA	10.9	46
GEORGIA	12.7	41
ARKANSAS	13.2	37
LOUISIANA	13.8	36
TENNESSEE	17.3	30
ALABAMA	18.2	28
SIMPLE AVERAGE OF PERCENTAGES IN NON-RIGHT-TO-WORK STATES	23.6%	
TOTAL UNITED STATES	21.9%	

Sources: U.S. Department of Commerce, Bureau of the Census, *National Data Book and Guide to Sources: Statistical Abstract of the United States*, 1988.

Moore and Newman (1985) review a number of studies regarding the effects of right–to–work laws and find that a great deal of controversy still exists. They conclude that the conflicting results reported by various authors are largely the result of different statistical approaches and the impreciseness of available data. They believe that the numerous studies have still not resolved the question of whether right–to–work laws repress levels of unionization or whether weak unions and negative public attitudes toward unions are the factors that lead to the passage of right–to–work laws in the first place.

Our research indicates that the existence of right–to–work laws conveys a message to investors about the union climate that exists in those states. The existence of right–to–work laws was a key factor in attracting 14 of the 20 companies in this study to Virginia and the Southeast. Nine executives cited the right–to–work laws as being "very important," and five others said they were "moderately important." Further exploration of the matter, however, made apparent that it was the low level of unionization in Virginia rather than right-to-work legislation per se that appealed to the executives. Many used the terms *right–to–work, low unionization,* and *labor climate* almost interchangeably.

As with wage rates, for the companies in our study, right–to–work laws seemed to be a more important factor in selecting a region than in selecting particular states. While only 10.9 percent of the nonagricultural work force is organized by labor unions in Virginia, ranking it 46th among the 50 states and the District of Columbia in this regard, Virginia's unionization level is still above that of certain other southeastern states.

Several companies in the study gave serious consideration to regions other than the Southeast, particularly the Northeast and Midwest, but the high level of unionization and the reputation for poor labor relations in those regions was discouraging. These executives were conditioned by difficult union experiences in the Northeast, and the goals of low unionization and good labor relations were particularly important to them. In some cases, union or right–to–work issues were important criteria which helped companies to choose among various southeastern states. For example, one executive stated,

> *We picked Virginia partly because it is the most northern of the right–to–work states.*

In at least one other case Virginia came out the winner, despite the following judgment made by an executive (in the context of favorable observations about right–to–work laws),

> *North Carolina has a better reputation for labor relations than Virginia.*

While the companies were attracted to the Southeast by right–to–work laws and a favorable labor climate, the interviews gave no indication that the companies were unwilling to work with unions. Indeed, a number of the European companies have strong unions in their home plants, with which they have good relations.

Land, Building, and Tax Costs

Executives in ten companies considered the cost of land, buildings, and taxes significant in the site selection process. Two viewed such costs as "very important" and eight as "moderately important." Real estate taxes and "personal property" taxes on equipment were the only taxes discussed.

Ordinarily, the cost of land was not a crucial factor in the decision process until the final stages, but there were exceptions. One company rejected possible locations along the Pacific Coast in Oregon and California because of high land costs. In another case, the initial search for a site in New Jersey was called off by the extraordinarily high costs of suitable land in the area of preference.

Land costs were ordinarily factored into the decision process in the following manner. First, in doing feasibility studies for their new U.S. manufacturing facilities, most companies established an acceptable range for land costs. Second, at the time different regions were considered, rough comparisons were made of approximate land costs, often based on subjective perceptions. Third, there was a presumption that a site with acceptable land costs would be found in some community or area. After a company decided to locate in the Southeast or some other region, land costs were not a critical "make–or–break" factor in selecting communities. Fourth, if there was more than one available site in the chosen community, land costs were often carefully compared.

In some instances, the eagerness of states and localities to attract foreign manufacturers led them to offer undeveloped land at very favorable prices. Commenting on this tendency, one executive stated,

> *Any state or locality will offer you a good deal on land. In fact, they'll virtually give you the land, just to get you into their area. As a result, land cost pretty much washed out in our site selection process. We only asked that the cost be competitive.*

Our interviews generated little conversation about building costs. Most of the companies selected land sites in industrial parks and constructed their buildings to specifications after the location decisions had been made. No one commented on the level of construction costs in Virginia as an inducement for locating in the state. As an indication of relative building costs, one executive found that lease rates for warehouses in central Virginia were much lower than in the Northeast.

Several companies did, however, buy existing buildings or structures. In one case, an executive was under considerable pressure to initiate U.S. operations as quickly as possible. By acquiring a preconstructed shell building in an industrial park, the company was able to save valuable time and facilitate financing.

A few companies referred to tax studies prepared internally or by the state economic development agency. In one case, a differential in tax rates between a city and the adjoining county was a pivotal issue leading the company to select a county location. Interestingly, not one company mentioned differences in utility costs — which other studies often considered a relevant cost factor.

Economic Incentives

Ten of the twenty companies were influenced in part by economic incentives offered by local communities or the state. These inducements were deemed "very important" by two companies and "moderately important" by eight. Financing assistance, industrial training services, screening of job applicants, and plant setup assistance were the economic incentives provided to the companies in our study. The following background on the use of economic incentives nationally will help put this experience in perspective.

The use of economic incentives to attract foreign investment to states and localities is a much–discussed topic among politicians and development officials, and the topic is not without controversy. Some states offer many and varied incentives to companies wishing to build new manufacturing facilities. In certain cases, they even give preferential treatment to foreign firms — incentives not available to domestic firms.

In the book *Buying Into America: How Foreign Money is Changing the Face of Our Nation,* authors Martin and Susan Tolchin explore the use of economic incentives to attract foreign manufacturing facilities:

> *The classic case of interstate rivalry involved the forty-state competition over the Volkswagen Rabbit plant. Although Ohio came close, Pennsylvania emerged the victor because it offered the most. The specific package included the following:*

- *A $40 million loan repayable in thirty years to purchase and build on to an unfinished former Chrysler plant. The interest rate averaged 4 percent, dipping down to 1.75 percent for the first twenty years.*

- *A $20 million bond issue for a road link between the plant and the state highway.*

- *A $10 million state bond issue for a railway spur linking the plant with a main line.*

- *A $6 million loan from the Pennsylvania state employees pension fund for fifteen years at 8.5 percent.*

- *A $3.8 million training program for Volkswagen workers, funded by the federal government but acquired through state efforts.*

- *A five–year county property tax abatement worth $200,000.*

- *State designation of the plant site as a foreign–trade subzone, bringing down the duty on finished cars to 3 percent.*

The total value of Pennsylvania's incentive package initially came to more than $51.7 million . . .

During the 1970s and 1980s, other multimillion–dollar incentive packages were offered by six mid–American states — Michigan, Ohio, Indiana, Illinois, Kentucky, and Tennessee — in the intense competition among states and communities to attract Japanese automobile assembly plants. Toyota, Mazda, Honda, Fuji-Isuzu, Mitsubishi, and Nissan all benefited from huge financial incentives that included tax abatements, state or local funding of infrastructure improvements (such as roads and sewers), and state absorption of employee training costs. The incentive programs were controversial with the principal attacks — even constitutional issues — being lodged by small business interests, labor unions, and environmentalists.

Although the incentive packages were substantial, it is not clear how much impact they had in influencing the final plant–location decisions by the Japanese automobile assemblers. The details of many packages have not been disclosed, but it is believed that more than one state made attractive overtures to each company.

Virginia and Indiana, both states with strong pro–investment stances, reflect sharp differences in policy regarding the use of incentives. According to Mark Akers, director of the Industrial Development division of the Indiana Department of Commerce, as reported in *Buying into America,*

We're not exactly a giveaway state. . .but we want to make sure companies do well once they're here. We help with tax abatement on buildings or equipment, with infrastructure, water, sewers and roads, and the state gives money to community loans.

Virginia development officials, although they court foreign firms actively, do not believe in offering significant economic incentives as a way of inducing foreign firms to locate there. In the Tolchin book, John Lenkey, III, former international director of the Virginia Department of Economic Development, summarized the state's philosophy regarding incentives this way,

In Virginia, there are no concessions to foreign firms. Our governor and tax commissioner won't play that game. It's not fair to our own (domestic) companies.

Table 3.7, compiled from data presented in the October, 1985 and October, 1986 issues of the *Industrial Development and Site Selection Handbook* , shows the major economic incentives offered by different states, the number of states proposing each incentive, and a comparison of the incentives offered by Indiana and Virginia. There is a similarity in the incentives offered by Indiana and Virginia, but Indiana offers six incentives that Virginia does not. Since the total dollar value of those incentives is not available, a direct financial comparison of the two state packages is impossible.

As shown in the table, incentives such as "State Recruiting and Screening of Industrial Employees" are offered by all 50 states. Others, such as "State Matching Funds for City or County Industrial Financing Programs," are offered by only a few. Overall, the table shows that the states in the Southeast, where the companies in our study concentrated their search, tend to offer fewer economic incentives to prospective companies than do states in other regions.

Note that the incentives shown in Table 3.7 are offered to both foreign and domestic firms. Most state legislation regarding incentives does not differentiate between the two sources. In practice, however, many states and localities use inducements on a discretionary basis to attract individual companies that are of particular interest. Such inducements may favor either foreign or domestic firms.

Economic and political realities may cause some states and localities to offer greater assistance to large companies than to small ones, because more new jobs are promised. In the case of Pennsylvania, for examle, the package offered to Volkswagen was far more generous than packages offered to smaller firms. Frequently states and localities will provide large employers with infrastructure improvements, including access roads and utility connections. Often these improvements are not offered to smaller employers.

Many states attract prospective investors with tax forgiveness — an economic incentive that establishes a partial or complete moratorium on tax payments for a specified length of time. Virginia laws do not permit the use of tax forgiveness. Instead, other economic incentives are used to attract companies. As noted previously, for the companies in our study, the types of economic incentives were low-cost financing, assistance in plant setup, screening of job applicants, and industrial training programs.

The most common financial incentives used by companies in our study were industrial development bonds (sometimes referred to as industrial revenue bonds). Programs involving these bonds are made possible by federal legislation and administered by the states. The bonds are generally issued by local governments, and the companies are provided with development funds and preferential interest rates from sale of the bonds. The interest income on industrial development bonds is exempt from federal and state income taxes. Several companies in the study used such bonds to finance land, plant, and equipment purchases.

As a result of recent changes in federal law, it is unlikely that the industrial development bond will continue to be a major financial incentive. First, the federal government has reduced the amount of funds that states and localities may raise by issuing industrial development bonds. Second, the tax-free treatment of interest income on industrial development bonds will end in 1990. Without the tax benefit, the bonds will be much less attractive to investors than they are now, and a source of new plant financing will be lost.

The Virginia Department of Economic Development is designing programs to replace industrial development bonds. The state also has a working capital loan–guarantee program allowing small businesses to borrow working-capital

Table 3.7

ECONOMIC INCENTIVES OFFERED BY STATES

FINANCIAL ASSISTANCE	NUMBER	INDIANA	VIRGINIA
State-Sponsored Industrial Development Authority	38	x	x
Privately Sponsored Development Credit Corp	36	x	
State Authority or Agency Revenue Bond Financing	42	x	x
State Authority General Obligation Bond Financing	12		
State Loans for Building Construction	35	x	
State Loans for Equipment and Machinery	34	x	
State Loan Guarantees for Building Construction	22	x	x
State Loan Guarantees for Equipment and Machinery	23	x	x
State Financing Aid for Existing Plant Expansion	38	x	
State Matching Funds for City and/or County Industrial Financing Programs	18	x	
State Incentives for Establishing Industrial Plants in Areas of High Unemployment	27	x	
TAX INCENTIVES			
Corporate Income Tax Exemption	33	x	
Excise Tax Exemption	18		
Tax Exemption or Moratorium on Land and Capital Improvements	34	x	a
Tax Exemption or Moratorium on Equipment and Machinery	35	b	a
Inventory Tax Exemption on Goods in Transit (Free Port)	47	c	d
Tax Exemption on Manufacturers' Inventories	44	c	x
Sales/Use Tax Exemption on New Equipment	42	x	x
Tax Exemption on Raw Materials Used in Manufacturing	45	x	x
Tax Incentive for Creation of New Jobs			
Tax Incentive for Industrial Investment	29	b	e
Tax Stabilization Agreements for Specified Industries	5		
Tax Exemption to Encourage Research and Development	24	x	f
Accelerated Depreciation of Industrial Equipment	34	x	x

Table 3.7 (continued)

ECONOMIC INCENTIVES OFFERED BY STATES

SPECIAL SERVICES FOR INDUSTRIAL DEVELOPMENT	NUMBER	INDIANA	VIRGINIA
State Industrial Revenue Bond Financing	50	x	x
State-Financed Speculative Building	13		
State Provides Free Land for Industry	2		
State-Owned Industrial Parks	10		
State Funds for City and/or County Master Plans	30	x	
State Program to Promote Research and Development	43	x	x
State Program to Increase Export of Products	50	x	x
University Research and Development Facilities Available to Industry	50	x	x
State- and/or University-Conducted Feasibility Studies to Attract New Industry	50	x	x
State Recruiting and Screening of Industrial Employees	50	x	x
State-Supported Training of Industrial Employees	50	x	x
State Retraining of Industrial Employees	49	x	x
State-Supported Training of "Hard-Core" Unemployed	43	x	
State Incentive to Private Industry to Train "Hard-Core" Unemployed	35	x	
State Science and/or Technology Advisory Council	45	x	x

a   In Virginia, localities have the option of totally or partially exempting certified pollution control or solar energy equipment.

b   Exemption is allowed on separate detachable accessories and equipment which have a useful life of less than 12 months.

c   Finished goods stored in public or private warehouses destined for out-of-state shipment are exempt.

d   Applies to imported goods if they have not lost their status as imports, to inventory which is imported or scheduled for export and is located in a foreign trade zone, and to manufacturers' inventory.

e   Applies to urban enterprise zones.

f   Local governments may classify separately the tangible personal property of R&D firms from that of other taxpayers and tax it at different rates. Sales and use tax exemptions are allowed for R&D.

Source: *Industrial Development and Site Selection Handbook, October, 1985 and October, 1986.*

funds. None of the companies in the study used the guaranteed working-capital loan program; they relied instead on working capital from their foreign parents.

Both state and local authorities provided certain types of financial assistance to some of the companies in the study. A number of local development agencies built industrial park sites and small buildings which they sold or leased to the companies. The use of existing industrial park facilities and shell buildings can lead to a considerable reduction in start-up time. When companies locate on undeveloped sites, the authorities can also provide assistance without making direct financial subsidies or granting tax forgiveness. For instance, we were informed by one executive that the state provided road access to the new plant, and the county installed sewer lines and other utilities.

A number of the companies took advantage of the job applicant screening program provided by the Virginia Employment Commission. In this program, Commission employees interview all job applicants and provide the company with a "short list" of qualified applicants. The final employee roster is selected from that list. Considering all of the complexities associated with setting up a new operation in a foreign country, managers are delighted to be relieved of the applicant-screening task. One executive noted that all of the states in the Southeast offered training programs as an incentive, and because these programs were roughly comparable, these factors "washed out" in the decision-making process.

For companies in our study, the Virginia Industrial Training Program was used more frequently than any other economic incentive. This program, directed by the Virginia Department of Economic Development, provides assistance for the training of new employees. Training sessions are conducted either by company employees or by qualified instructors provided by the state. The state also reimburses companies for selected travel expenses when company personnel are sent overseas to the home plant for training. One service of the Department of Economic Development that proved particularly useful was assistance in the production of training videos. Four companies took advantage of this service.

The economic development officials we interviewed in Virginia and North Carolina believed that company executives were reasonably adept at playing off one state against another to obtain the best possible package of incentives. Financial incentives offered by one state were quickly matched by those in another, particularly among states in the Southeast. As a consequence, economic incentives tended to be fairly similar across the region. Rather than promoting economic incentives, therefore, economic development officials tended to promote other desirable location factors, such as labor availability and wages, right–to–work laws, seaports and highways—advantages that made their states attractive places in which to construct and operate new manufacturing plants.

There are cases, of course, in which states offer incentives so attractive that companies accept the offer before other states have had an opportunity to make a counteroffer. Moreover, as evidenced in the Volkswagen example, states competing for significant investments can bid the total value of incentive packages to extraordinarily high levels. The companies in our study had not had that experience.

Evidence in the literature corroborates our findings that financial incentives are not usually critical factors in the site selection process. In the December, 1981, issue of *Federal Reserve Bank of Atlanta Economic Review* Jeffrey S. Arpan examined the importance of economic incentives in site selections by foreign investors and reached the following conclusion:

> *Despite the recent explosion in promotional activities. . .current research suggests that foreign investors do not consider incentives as important as the overall investment climate in a state.*

Arpan then discussed two recent studies of site selection factors, including a study by Bernard Imbert of French companies that had invested in the Southeast:

> *Imbert studied the southeastern investments of 16 French companies, and, among other topics, asked for a ranking of the most important factors that influenced the companies to locate in the Southeast and in the particular state. Inducements and incentives of state and local authorities ranked eleventh out of sixteen factors, and were ranked as a "major" factor by only two firms, and an "important" factor by only two other firms.*

Arpan noted that the findings of a study by G. Lynn Derrick of German investments in South Carolina were similar to those of Imbert:

> *As was the case with French investors, incentives of state and local authorities were not ranked as critical factors.*

Thus, evidence in the literature confirms that economic incentives are not ordinarily critical in the site selection process. Financial incentives were important for a number of companies in our study, but they were not compelling factors.

Economic Development Agencies

Twelve of the 20 executives in our study pointed to the significant role played by economic development agencies in the site selection process. Five saw the role as "very important," and seven viewed the role as "moderately important." Several executives stated that the enthusiasm, dedication, and professionalism of state and local officials was a critical element in their choice of a location.

The role of these agencies can be understood through a review of the topic from a national perspective. Robert H. Pittman, in the August, 1985, *Industrial Development and Site Selection Handbook,* notes that there are 5,345 state and local economic development agencies in the United States. The number of agencies per state varies greatly, however, ranging from a high of 335 in Texas to a low of 4 in Kansas. Virginia, with 169 agencies, is somewhat above the national average of 107.

According to Pittman, these agencies may be classified into three groups:

1. public agencies sponsored by state, county, or municipal governments,
2. private, nonprofit agencies such as chambers of commerce and economic development associations,
3. divisions or offices in private companies, including banks, railroads, and utilities.

Public agencies promote economic development as a matter of public policy. There are 1,700 public agencies nationwide, comprising 32.1 percent of all such agencies. The private, nonprofit agencies which promote general business activities number 2,737 — 51.7 percent of all economic development agencies. Divisions or offices in private companies carry out economic development activities to enhance their own business and to improve the business climate in their communities. Private companies engaging in economicdevelopment activities number 858, or 16.2 percent of all such agencies. The largest and most influential agencies are the 50 state offices of economic development. In 1985, these public agencies operated with an average staff of 109 employees and an average annual budget of $7.8 million.

The development of international business is a high priority of the state economic development agencies. Almost all of the states appropriate funds for international business development, ranging from $25,000 annually in Idaho to $5.7 million in California, according to 1986 figures from the National Association of State Development Agencies. Virginia ranks 13th nationally, with an international budget of $900,000. There is a broad range in the staffing for international activities. Minnesota has 41 employees and Nevada has just one employee devoted part-time to the subject. Virginia again ranks 13th nationally, with 14 employees in its international division.

Virginia became the first state to open an overseas economic development office when its Port Authority set up an office in Brussels in 1955. Since then, 31 states have established foreign offices in 22 different cities. The most popular locations for overseas development offices are: Tokyo (offices from 20 states), Brussels (8), London (6), Frankfurt (5), and Hong Kong (3). Düsseldorf, Mexico City, Seoul, and Toronto each have two state offices.

The focal point for all economic development activity in Virginia is the State Department of Economic Development based in Richmond. The department has as its mission

To encourage, stimulate, and support the economic development of the Commonwealth by.   .maintaining and promoting an attractive business climate which will assist the expansion of the economy of Virginia.

In addition to its main office in Richmond, the department maintains regional offices in Abingdon (southwest Virginia), Staunton (Shenandoah Valley), and South Boston (south central Virginia). The department also maintains overseas offices in Brussels and Tokyo. Altogether, the Department of Economic Development operated with a staff of 71 and an annual budget of $6.3 million in 1986.

The 168 local development agencies in Virginia vary considerably in size. One of the largest, Forward Hampton Roads, coordinates the marketing efforts of five cities in the Tidewater area (Chesapeake, Norfolk, Portsmouth, Suffolk, and Virginia Beach). Its annual budget of $550,000 covers the salaries of eight employees, promotional trips to other countries, advertisements in numerous business publications, and the agency's participation in the annual Hanover, West Germany, Trade Fair. Internal marketing efforts generated 49 percent of the company contacts handled by Forward Hampton Roads in 1987. The State Department of Economic Development provided another 45 percent, and referrals from such other organizations as the Virginia Port Authority and local chambers of commerce originated the remaining six percent.

The Industrial Development Authority of Louisa County is typical of small development agencies. Located in a rural area 45 miles west of Richmond, the Louisa County agency employs a full-time secretary and an economic development consultant who works an average of two days a week. Louisa County has limited funds for journal advertising or for promotional trips. The Authority relies on the State Department of Economic Development for 80 to 90 percent of its contacts with prospective companies. A large industrial park in Louisa County, which features an adjoining airport suitable for corporate aircraft, was financed by the Authority. The park is the Authority's main promotional tool. Like Forward Hampton Roads, Louisa County has been successful in bringing foreign manufacturing companies into its territory.

The State Department of Economic Development plays an important role in plant-location decisions by foreign companies. Prospective foreign investors (called "clients" by development officials) contact the department through either its Richmond office or its overseas offices in Brussels or Tokyo. Why these companies sometimes initiate discussions with economic development officials in Richmond and sometimes with officials abroad is not always clear. In this study, Sumitomo Machinery relied on managers from its New Jersey location to contact the Richmond office. Canon, on the other hand, elected to approach the Tokyo office of the Virginia Department of Economic Development and relied on managers from its headquarters in Japan to make the contact — although Canon has maintained sales and marketing offices in the United States for a long time and is, presumably, familiar with the Richmond office.

After contact, the Department of Economic Development assigns a marketing representative to work with the client. The company is sent a questionnaire requesting information on its plant-location requirements, which would include details on acreage, factory size, labor force needs, utilities, special infrastructure requirements, transportation, and the type of community desired. The marketing representative from the department matches company requirements against a comprehensive data base, which lists available sites throughout the state. The data base of sites is maintained by department employees from information supplied mainly by local development officials, who provide updates on the available sites in their communities.

From the data base, the marketing representative chooses several sites (generally four to six) that appear to meet the company's needs. To help the client evaluate the sites, the representative often prepares detailed comparisons of the sites' characteristics, including land and construction costs, average wage rates, employee education levels, nearby technical schools and colleges, utility and tax rates, housing and living costs, recreational opportunities, and other details about the locations. Similar information is sometimes compiled that compares Virginia attributes, such as property taxes, with those of other states.

A tour of the sites is then arranged (using the governor's airplane if the sites under consideration are located in different areas of the state). The tour encourages considerable interaction and cooperation between State and local economic development officials. Once a distinct interest is shown in a particular location, local economic development officials assume the prime responsibility for working with the foreign client to negotiate the many details of site selection. State officials continue to play a facilitating role throughout these negotiations, but local officials remain in charge until contracts are signed and construction begins. Companies occasionally bypass the state Department of Economic Development and contact local agencies directly. In such circumstances, local officials ordinarily keep State officials informed regarding the status of negotiations.

There are both similarities and differences in the way North Carolina and Virginia handle their economic development activities. The North Carolina agency, known for its success in attracting foreign manufacturing investment, began operations in 1937. It consists of a head office in Raleigh, eight regional offices around the state, and foreign offices in Düsseldorf, West Germany, and in Tokyo. Marketing representatives in North Carolina and in Virginia perform similar functions, with two notable exceptions. In North Carolina, representatives from the state office remain in charge throughout the entire site selection process, and North Carolina uses state development funds to advertise specific, privately owned industrial sites in development periodicals.

Our interviews indicate that the work of economic development agencies and the interaction of state and local officials make strong impressions on company executives. A number of executives commented on how effectively state and local employees worked together and how enthusiastic and attentive they had been. In one case, the ability of state and county development authorities to put together a comprehensive site-development package within 30 days led directly to the company's decision to locate in Virginia. The package included land, building, utility, infrastructure, and financing considerations.

In summary, the cooperative work of state and local economic development officials conveyed attitudes of professionalism and enthusiasm to the clients. As a result, the foreign executives in this study felt comfortable about Virginia and their decision to locate in the state.

Quality of Life

Executives in ten of the 20 companies studied cited quality–of–life factors as being significant in the location decision — three citing the considerations as being "very important" and seven as "moderately important." The interviews revealed, however, that quality of life entered the thinking of most other executives as well. Judgments about quality of life played a prominent role in the selection of regions, states, and specific communities.

Quality of life is an indicator of how certain characteristics of an area affect the personal lives of the workers in that area. There is no standard definition for the term, but the concept encompasses educational opportunities, the climate, cultural advantages, recreational facilities, proximity to the mountains or the seas, and attractiveness of neighborhoods.

The importance of quality of life in firms' location decisions in general is highlighted in the *Industrial Development and Site Selection Handbook's* annual "Geo–Life" survey. The August, 1987, survey, based on questionnaire responses from 280 development directors in the United States, Canada, and other countries, concludes,

> *What makes QOL [quality of life] so important to corporate facility planners? In short, it's the bottom line, with two factors looming the largest: recruitment and relocation. All else being equal, it is easier to recruit personnel for less money or to recruit better qualified people for the same pay to a location with a high quality of life. By the same token, it's easier to transfer or relocate present employees to a location with a high quality of life.*

The company executives in our study who cited quality of life as a factor were concerned about providing favorable working and living environments for managers and employees, particularly those employees relocated from home countries. Frequently, difficulties were encountered in inducing employees to leave home countries to live overseas, in spite of pay raises, promotions, and other enticements. The prospect of an attractive living environment was thus seen as an important factor in persuading foreign nationals to relocate.

The importance of quality–of–life factors is illustrated by the experience of one Japanese company which was relocating a number of Japanese nationals to its new facility in the United States. Company officials believed the problems of relocation and cultural adjustment might be minimized if they found a location somewhat reminiscent of Japan. Southeastern Virginia, with its moderate, humid climate and proximity to the ocean, was more similar to Tokyo than any of the other regions considered. In addition, the Tidewater area offered cross-cultural programs in universities and special "Saturday Schools" in its elementary schools for foreigners. These educational activities were organized to help employees and their families adjust to life in Virginia. During the search, company executives gave this Virginia location high marks for its quality of life, and that became a strong consideration in the final decision.

Managers were concerned with quality of life not just for their current and prospective employees, but also for themselves. One executive considered Maryland, in part, because his wife's family lived there. Another executive, an avid sailor, was particularly attracted to a specific site because of its proximity to the water. Several managers listed the positive attributes of their locations, citing their own personal preferences, such as:

I like the cultural amenities of this community.

It's great to live in a climate where I can enjoy golf nearly all year round.

Based on our research, we conclude that the personal preferences of foreign executives, particularly the decision makers, play an important role in the location process.

Business Climate

Four executives in the study mentioned the business climate of a state or locality as a "moderately important" factor in the site selection process. Several other executives implied through their comments that the business climate associated with a location was a consideration.

In the interviews, the term *business climate* was used to describe the suitability of the business environment within a state or community, as perceived by executives. Reflecting attitudes about the environment rather than specific quantifiable factors, the assessment of the *business climate* is the net effect of many qualitative judgments, including:

- the degree of enthusiasm about businesses demonstrated by community residents

- the amount of help given to prospective businesses by bankers, other professionals, and fellow business people

- the measure of harmony or acrimony surrounding labor relations in the community

- the attitudes of legislators toward business, as reflected by the laws and regulations governing or constraining business activities

- the attitudes of state and local officials toward business, as indicated by the degree of toughness or leniency shown in enforcing laws and ensuring compliance with regulations

- the presence or absence of anti-business activist or pressure groups

- the favorable or unfavorable actions of state or local governing boards on matters of growth planning, zoning, environmental control, and other issues

The term *business climate* is often used interchangeably with the terms *manufacturing climate* and *investment climate*. In the literature, however, there are discernible differences among these terms.

An example of *manufacturing climate* may be found in the *Ninth Annual Grant Thornton Manufacturing Climates Study*. In this report, the manufacturing climate of each state is calculated using 21 quantitative factors grouped into five major categories:

1. fiscal policies of state and local governments
2. state-regulated employment costs
3. labor costs
4. availability and productivity of resources
5. selected quality-of-life issues (education, health care, cost of living, and transportation)

The factors are measured, weighted, and totaled to form a composite state factor value. The states are then ranked. In our discussions with economic development officials in North Carolina, they referred to the Grant Thornton state rankings, in which North Carolina ranked third among the 27 states with "high manufacturing intensity." The officials cited the high ranking as evidence that North Carolina is an attractive business location. Interestingly, the survey ranked Virginia sixth among the 22 states of "low manufacturing intensity."

An example of the term *investment climate* may be found in the *Federal Reserve Board of Atlanta Economic Journal* December, 1981, issue. *Investment climate* was defined as an amalgam of these factors:

1. logistics (transportation)
2. labor
3. utilities (availability and cost)
4. construction
5. financial
6. lifestyle

We cannot be sure of the exact meaning of "business climate" as it was used by the executives in our study. One executive noted the helpful, positive attitudes of the bankers, lawyers, businesspeople, and community residents he met in Virginia. These attitudes reflecting the business climate had a very positive effect on his final decision.

Nearness to Home Country

Executives in five companies — four European and one Canadian — felt it was important to find a U.S. location as close to their home country as possible. As a consequence, executives in the four European companies limited their search to locations along the Atlantic coast. From a business perspective, locating close to Europe would minimize travel time and expense and cut down on jet lag. Telephone communications to Europe are more convenient than they are from more westerly time zones. Relocation costs from Europe are lower than they would be to inland or West Coast points. From a psychological standpoint, managers along the Atlantic coast "feel" close to home and to the headquarters of the parent company, which enhances parent-subsidiary unity.

From a quality–of–life perspective, an Atlantic coast location helps European employees cope with the adjustment inherent in living in the United States. Shorter travel times to and from Europe make employees feel less isolated from home. In addition, many cities along the Atlantic coast are home to large numbers of expatriate Europeans, which gives newcomers greater opportunity for association with compatriots. These benefits contribute to an enjoyable quality of life and to greater job satisfaction for European workers.

Executives in the Canadian company limited their search to locations within one day's driving time of their Canadian headquarters.

Special Climatic Conditions

Six of the 20 companies conducted their search with special climatic conditions in mind, and these environmental requirements were "very important" in four instances and "moderately important" in two. The following examples indicate why special climatic conditions were sought. Two of the companies needed hot and humid summers with moderate winters to help in the proper aging of their food products. An electronics firm required a location that was free from airborne corrosive salts. This need eliminated a location close to the ocean. A vineyard and wine corporation decided to locate in a particular section of the Virginia Piedmont that enjoys a long growing season, cool summer nights, and mild winters — conditions favorable for the growth of French wine grapes.

Proximity to Competitors

It was "very important" for one company to find a location that was near the facilities of its principal competitors, which was seen as a way of enhancing market visibility. The company wanted to establish itself as a prime participant in its market.

Joint Ventures

Two companies, each owned jointly by two foreign parents, had a strong preference for locating near an established U.S. plant of a parent. For operational and management reasons, a location in close proximity to a parent was "very important" for these joint venture companies. Although such a location was not an absolute requirement, it ultimately shaped the decision.

Virginia History and Culture

Two companies found the history and culture of Virginia "very important" as a site selection consideration. The Japanese owners of one company were the seventh generation of a family that managed the firm. The company operated in an industry that was over a thousand years old. To executives in this company, the relatively long history of settlement in Virginia and the state's historical importance were very appealing. Executives from an Italian company felt comfortable with Virginia for the same reasons.

Positioning of Additional Plants

Similarly, for two companies that had other established U.S. manufacturing operations at the time of the location search, finding a new site that fit logistically with the existing plants was "very important." A Southeast location was a strategic choice, made after considering markets, raw material availability, and existing plants.

Distance From Residential Housing

One chemical company considered it "very important" to have a plant location fairly distant from any residential communities. This thinking recognized environmental realities and was intended to anticipate community feelings.

SUMMARY

The managerial process involved in site selection by foreign companies usually involves the choice of a geographic region, the selection of two or more states in that region, and, finally, the careful examination of several sites in each state. Contrary to much conventional wisdom, foreign companies seldom decide on one particular state for their manufacturing operations. The final decision on a state is determined by the attributes of particular sites or communities. There are, however, aberrations and variations to this pattern, with some companies narrowly restricting their search to a specific community.

The site selection process is driven by personal and emotional factors as well as company interests—particularly in family-owned, private companies where one person, the owner, can immediately approve or veto any site. The same subjective tendencies are also present in publicly owned corporations, however.

The companies have criteria (in the form of location factors) for regions, states, communities, and specific sites. We encountered few rigorous factor-by-factor analyses for regions, however, and even fewer for particular states. Executives were strongly influenced by preconceptions they had about the advantages and disadvantages of various areas. As far as we could tell, the preconceptions tended to be partially or completely correct. Most of the detailed analyses, when they were done, were reserved for the decisions on specific sites.

For the executives in our study, the desire to be close to markets was the most important single factor affecting the location decision. A moderate union climate, symbolized by right-to-work laws, was also extremely important. The ready accessibility of an excellent seaport was a key magnet as well.

Officials in economic development agencies play an instrumental role in the site selection process. They suggest specific sites for consideration, organize tours, and prepare relevant cost analyses. The diligence and professionalism of state and local officials was an influential factor in a number of site location decisions.

Economic incentives and land, building, and tax costs had less overall impact on the decisions. State-sponsored employee training programs, pre–employment screening of employees, and financing assistance through industrial development bonds were persuasive. Land costs were important for a few companies in choosing among alternate sites in a chosen community.

Unusual factors can be extremely significant for particular companies. We encountered the need for very specific climatic requirements, the desire to be near the plants of parent companies, the search for a site near competitors, and a requirement that a plant be distant from any residential community.

The implications for economic development officials, state and local legislators, government administrators, and business managers of the findings in this part are given in the summary and conclusions of the book.

PART 4

EXPERIENCES OF
INDIVIDUAL COMPANIES

This part provides a brief description of 19 of the 20 companies in the study and reviews the investment and plant-location decision processes in each of these firms. As noted earlier, one company elected to maintain its anonymity because of company policies. This company has been retained in all aggregate data of the study.

For the other 19 companies, information is presented about each company's product line, the character of its manufacturing operations, its size, the nature and nationality of its parent company, and the community where the facility is located. The sequence of each company's investment and site selection decision is then given.

As noted in the introduction, no attempt was made to structure our sample in a way that would approximate some universe, such as all foreign affiliates in Virginia, all foreign affiliates in the United States, or all manufacturing establishments. We concentrated on recent entrants or plant announcements (16 of the 20 plants commenced operations in the 1986–88 period). We also tended to avoid small companies, those with fewer than ten employees.

The 20 companies in the study manufactured a diversified range of products in a number of industries. As indicated in Table 4.1, four companies were in the food and kindred products industry, four in the machinery industry, and four in the electrical and electronics products industry — 20 percent of the study companies in each of these three industries. The concentration of our sample in these industries is much greater than the comparable percentages for such establishments (domestic and foreign) in Virginia or in the United States. The percentage of machinery and electronics plants in our sample is, however, roughly equivalent to the percentage of such foreign-affiliate establishments in Virginia as a whole.

The companies in the study vary greatly in size, from an affiliate with five employees to one with 550 employees. Table 4.2 shows an array of the companies broken down by number of employees. Comparable data are presented for foreign and domestic establishments in the United States overall and in Virginia. Only two of the foreign affiliates in the survey, or ten percent, have more than 250 employees.

Table 4.1

NUMBER OF MANUFACTURING ESTABLISHMENTS BY INDUSTRY: UNITED STATES, VIRGINIA, AND TWENTY COMPANIES IN THE STUDY

NUMBER OF ESTABLISHMENTS	FOOD AND KINDRED PRODUCTS	FURNITURE AND FIXTURES	CHEMICALS AND ALLIED PRODUCTS	MACHINERY AND EQUIPMENT	ELECTRONIC AND ELECTRICAL EQUIPMENT	OTHER	TOTAL
UNITED STATES FOREIGN AND DOMESTIC OWNERS	22,130	10,003	11,901	52,912	16,453	244,662	358,061
VIRGINA							
ALL ESTABLISHMENTS	445	182	166	526	190	4,059	5,568
FOREIGN AFFILIATES ONLY	7	4	15	28	23	66	143
STUDY COMPANIES	4	2	1	4	4	5	20
PERCENT OF TOTAL							
UNITED STATES FOREIGN AND DOMESTIC OWNERS	6.2%	2.8%	3.3%	14.8%	4.6%	68.3%	100.0%
VIRGINIA							
ALL ESTABLISHMENTS	8.0	3.3	3.0	9.4	3.4	72.9	100.0
FOREIGN AFFILIATES ONLY	4.9	2.8	10.5	19.6	16.1	46.1	100.0
STUDY COMPANIES	20.0	10.0	5.0	20.0	20.0	25.0	100.0

Note: Total establishments in the United States and Virginia as of 1982. Virginia foreign affiliates as of January, 1987.
Source: U.S. Department of Commerce, Bureau of the Census, 1982 Census of Manufactures; Commonwealth of Virginia, Department of Economic Development, International Marketing, *Foreign Affiliated Virginia Firms*.

Table 4.2

SIZE OF MANUFACTURING ESTABLISHMENTS: UNITED STATES, VIRGINIA, AND THE TWENTY COMPANIES IN THE STUDY

(size determined by number of employees)

NUMBER OF EMPLOYEES	NUMBER OF ESTABLISHMENTS			PERCENT OF TOTAL		
	UNITED STATES FOREIGN & DOMESTIC	VIRGINIA FOREIGN & DOMESTIC	STUDY COMPANIES	UNITED STATES FOREIGN & DOMESTIC	VIRGINIA FOREIGN & DOMESTIC	STUDY COMPANIES
1 – 9	164,725	2,643	1	46.0%	47.5%	5.0%
10 – 49	116,597	1,733	7	32.5	31.1	35.0
50 – 99	28,563	448	6	8.0	8.0	30.0
100 – 249	22,463	428	4	6.3	7.7	20.0
over 250	25,713	316	2	7.2	5.7	10.0
TOTAL	358,061	5,568	20	100.0%	100.0%	100.0%

Source: U.S. Department of Commerce, Bureau of the Census, *1982 Census of Manufactures.*

The corresponding percentages for all manufacturing establishments in the United States and Virginia are much lower, 3.6 and 5.7 percent respectively. Only five percent of the companies in our sample have nine or fewer employees, compared with 49.5 percent in the United States and 47.5 percent in Virginia. Most of the companies in the study have imposing manufacturing operations, but they are not labor-intensive, and they are not giant manufacturing establishments.

The 20 foreign affiliates in the study are owned by companies with home offices in ten different foreign countries. As seen in Table 4.3, Japanese companies have the largest representation, owning the equivalent of 4.5 facilities (Japanese companies own four subsidiaries outright, and they own a 50 percent interest in a joint venture). The nation with the second largest ownership interest in the studied companies is West Germany, with Switzerland third. In the case of Japan, West Germany, and Switzerland, the ownership percentages in our study are well above those for all foreign affiliates in Virginia and in the United States generally. Correspondingly, the percentage of ownership of the companies represented by Canada and the United Kingdom is well below comparable figures for Virginia and the United States.

The plants of the 20 companies in the study are located across much of the state of Virginia. As shown in Figure 4.1, most facilities are concentrated in metropolitan areas, with seven plants located in the Richmond/Colonial Heights area alone. The Tidewater metropolitan area — Norfolk, Newport News, Suffolk, Chesapeake, and Hampton with its deepwater seaport — contains five of these plants. There are two plants in the southern part of the state (in Danville and South Boston). Southwest Virginia does not have any representation at all, and there is only one facility in northern Virginia (in Springfield).

The decision sequence provided for each company briefly outlines the investment and site selection decision-making processes. Each sequence recounts the circumstances surrounding the decision to manufacture in the United States and traces the stages and analyses involved in the site selection. Careful review of the individual decision sequences reveals the extent to which the decisions were conditioned by company-specific criteria and by personal circumstances. Yet certain broad patterns are evident — choice of a geographic region, selection of two or three states in that region, and identification of four to six sites in each state. These patterns were discussed in some detail in Part 3 in the section entitled "Managerial Process."

Table 4.3

HOME COUNTRIES OF FOREIGN AFFILIATES:
UNITED STATES, VIRGINIA, AND THE TWENTY COMPANIES IN THE STUDY

ALL INDUSTRIES
(Manufacturing and Nonmanufacturing)

COUNTRY	NUMBER OF FOREIGN AFFILIATES			PERCENT OF TOTAL		
	UNITED STATES	VIRGINIA	STUDY COMPANIES	UNITED STATES	VIRGINIA	STUDY COMPANIES
CANADA	1,324	64	1.0	13.7%	11.4%	5.0%
FRANCE	483	39	1.0	5.0	7.0	5.0
WEST GERMANY	1,305	83	4.0	13.5	14.8	20.0
UNITED KINGDOM	1,087	102	1.0	11.2	18.2	5.0
SWITZERLAND	761	42	3.0	7.9	7.5	15.0
JAPAN	902	24	4.5	9.3	4.3	22.5
OTHER	3,807	206	5.5	39.4	36.8	27.5
TOTAL	9,669	560	20.0	100.0%	100.0%	100.0%

Source: U.S. Department of Commerce, Bureau of Economic Analysis, *Foreign Direct Investment in the U.S.: Operations of U.S. Affiliates of Foreign Companies (Preliminary 1986 Estimates)*.

Figure 4.1

LOCATION OF PARTICIPATING COMPANIES

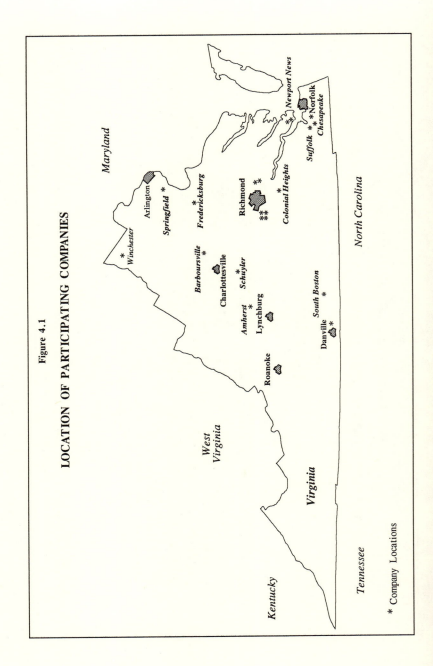

* Company Locations

COMPANY PROFILES
and
DECISION SEQUENCES

ALLIED COLLOIDS INC.

PROFILE OF THE U.S. COMPANY

HOME COUNTRY OF PARENT

United Kingdom

PRODUCT

The company produces water- soluble polymers for use in a number of industries, including petroleum, paper, textiles, and selected minerals. Other major uses for the product are in agriculture, pollution control, and specialized surface coatings.

NUMBER OF EMPLOYEES

160 on-site, 220 total

OPERATIONS

The Virginia facility produces 40 percent of the product sold by the company in the United States. The remainder are imported from the United Kingdom. The production facility uses continuous-flow process technology. The Virginia facility also has a state-of-the-art research laboratory.

SIZE

The company operates in a 50,000-square-foot complex on a 70-acre site. Initial plant and related investment costs were $65 million. A $15 million expansion was undertaken in 1988.

PARENT COMPANY

Allied Colloids PLC is a publicly traded British company based in Bradford, West Yorkshire. The company has manufacturing and sales operations in the United States and the United Kingdom, with marketing operations in eight other countries.

LOCATION AND COMMUNITY

Suffolk is one of several communities that make up the Tidewater metropolitan area. The northern boundary of Suffolk adjoins the harbor of Hampton Roads. The southern area of Suffolk is in the Great Dismal Swamp. The port of Hampton Roads is a critical element in the economics of the Tidewater area. With 409 square miles, Suffolk is the largest incorporated area in Virginia. It has a population of 50,000 and is the least densely populated city in the state.

ALLIED COLLOIDS — DECISION SEQUENCE

THE DECISION TO MANUFACTURE IN THE UNITED STATES

The cost of producing products in the United States for U.S. sales was lower than the cost of exporting from the U.K., principally because transatlantic transportation costs were eliminated.

At the time of the decision (1980), foreign currency exchange rates favored a U.S. location (the dollar was low relative to the pound, based on historical levels).

SELECTING A SPECIFIC SITE

At the outset, the company was predisposed to build the new plant at a specific site near its New Jersey sales and distribution facility.

The site purchase could not be negotiated, however, so the company decided to expand the scope of its search for a suitable site.

SELECTION OF SPECIFIC GEOGRAPHIC REGIONS AND STATES

A systematic search was conducted in states along the Atlantic coast.

Requests for site information were sent to economic development agencies in New Jersey, New York, Pennsylvania, Virginia, and North Carolina.

Only Virginia and North Carolina responded quickly, showing significant interest.

Company interest in Virginia and North Carolina was reinforced by concern about unionization in northern states.

FINAL SITE SELECTION

The company worked with both state and local development agencies in Virginia and North Carolina, touring several prospective sites in each state.

Sites were evaluated on the basis of three major factors:
- proximity to deepwater port
- quality of life
- remoteness of site from housing and residential areas

After careful consideration, the company chose the site in Suffolk, Virginia.

BARBOURSVILLE VINEYARDS

PROFILE OF THE U.S. COMPANY

HOME COUNTRY OF PARENT

Italy

SIZE

Operations are conducted on an 830-acre farm, of which 50 acres are planted with grapevines.

PRODUCT

The company's winery produces five varietal white and blush wines, two varietal red wines, and one generic wine. Production in 1986 was 19,000 U.S. gallons or 8,000 cases.

PARENT COMPANY

Zonin S.p.A. is the largest private winery in Italy. Its total turnover in 1985 was 50 billion lire (approximately $26 million). In Italy, the company employs 200 people and has the capacity to produce

NUMBER OF EMPLOYEES

10

OPERATIONS

Grapes grown in the Barboursville vineyards are crushed in a modern winery, which was improved and expanded in 1988. Wine is stored and aged in stainless steel tanks and red oak barrels, with a total capacity of 75,000 U.S. gallons.

LOCATION AND COMMUNITY

Barboursville Vineyards is located in a rural area near Charlottesville on the former Barboursville Plantation. The plantation was originally owned by statesman James Barbour, who served as Virginia governor from 1812 to 1814. The site is a registered Virginia Historic Landmark and includes the imposing, picturesque ruins of Governor Barbour's mansion. The mansion, gutted by fire on Christmas Day, 1886, was designed by Thomas Jefferson. The rolling countryside surrounding Barboursville has traditionally been the home of horse- and cattle-breeding estates. Several other vineyards have been established in the region in recent years.

BARBOURSVILLE VINEYARDS
DECISION SEQUENCE

THE DECISION TO MANUFACTURE IN THE UNITED STATES

The Zonin family owned several Italian wineries, and their company had been exporting Italian wines to the United States.

The company wanted to expand its market share in the United States with a domestic wine label.

$\downarrow$

SELECTION OF SPECIFIC GEOGRAPHIC REGIONS AND STATES

The Zonin company maintained a passive interest in the possibility of owning a vineyard and winery in wine-growing states, including California, New York, and Virginia.

$\downarrow$

FINAL SITE SELECTION

A British business group acted as brokers for the 800-acre Barbour estate. They approached the Zonins and convinced them of the attractiveness of the estate for establishing a vineyard.

The following factors were instrumental in management thinking regarding the purchase of the Barbour estate, a farm with viticultural possibilities:

- The climate was acceptable for growing wine grapes.

- The Zonin family was attracted by the historical aspects of growing wine grapes in the Virginia Piedmont region, a dream of Thomas Jefferson.

- The family was also impressed by the farm's history. It had been owned by an early Virginia governor, James Barbour. The ruins of the Barbour mansion, designed by Jefferson, are still on the property.

CANON VIRGINIA, INC.

PROFILE OF THE U.S. COMPANY

HOME COUNTRY OF PARENT

Japan

PRODUCT

The company manufactures photocopiers and laser printers that are marketed under the Canon name, and original equipment for other computer companies such as Hewlett Packard.

NUMBER OF EMPLOYEES

596 as of June 30, 1988

OPERATIONS

The operation in Virginia involves the assembly of office machines and computer equipment from parts and components. Some 1,500 different components are needed to make one copier, and overseas parts are imported through the port of Seattle, mainly from Japan. Three of Canon's suppliers in Japan have already set up facilities in Virginia in order to supply the new Canon factory. Canon Virginia would like an increasing proportion of its components to come from domestic sources. One of the features of the production process is the emphasis on quality.

SIZE

Manufacturing operations are conducted on a 168-acre site with a 292,000-square-foot factory. The initial investment was $26 million, expected to increase to between $100 million and $125 million within 5 years.

PARENT COMPANY

Canon, the parent, is the world's second largest manufacturer of plain paper copiers, with confirmed worldwide revenues of $5.5 billion and U.S. revenues of $3.4 billion. Sales in Canon's business machine segment represented 74 percent of consolidated sales. Founded 48 years ago as a camera manufacturer, Canon is now the world's largest producer of 35 mm cameras. Canon is a diversified multinational corporation with 69 percent of its sales overseas. In 1985, Canon manufactured products on three continents and had sales in more than 130 countries. More than one-third of the company's 36,000 employees are foreign nationals.

LOCATION AND COMMUNITY

Newport News, with a population of 157,000, is located at the mouth of the James River on the north side of Hampton Roads, the nation's largest natural harbor. The city's economy is based on shipbuilding and repair, manufacturing, seafood, and tourism.

CANON VIRGINIA— DECISION SEQUENCE

THE DECISION TO MANUFACTURE IN THE UNITED STATES

Canon had a global manufacturing strategy and wanted to establish manufacturing operations in the United States and Europe, as well as in Japan, in order to become one of the world's largest makers of copiers, as well as of other business equipment. The Canon management also believed that locations in various countries would help the company design products that were attuned to the needs of the different markets.

The foreign-currency exchange rate between the dollar and the yen made it advantageous to manufacture in the United States rather than to export from Japan.

The possibility of increased trade barriers and tariffs in the future threatened the viability of exporting copiers from Japan to the United States.

With concern about Japanese-American trade imbalances and the possibility of a backlash, Canon managers viewed manufacturing in the United States as a positive, corrective action.

$\downarrow$

SELECTION OF SPECIFIC GEOGRAPHIC REGIONS AND STATES

In 1980, Canon sent a delegation to the United States to study location prospects.

The site search was focused on the Southeast region for six reasons:

- Canon already had a facility in California. The East Coast was a strategic location for serving the eastern market.
- A moderate climate was needed to use the Just-In-Time inventory method, with its emphasis on minimal inventories and precise delivery schedules. Snow and bad weather would delay deliveries and raise employee absenteeism. Also, a moderate climate similar to the climate in Japan was seen as an advantage, by making it easier for Japanese employees to adjust to life in a foreign land.
- The region had a reputation for progressive, high-technology industrial development.
- Wage rates were attractive relative to other regions.
- Unitary corporate income taxes could be avoided.
- The region was known for its productive employees and its friendly community relations.

$\downarrow$

FINAL SITE SELECTION

In 1985, a second site-selection delegation visited 100 sites in Georgia, North Carolina, Virginia, and Maryland.

The choice was narrowed to five sites, two in Virginia and one in each of the other states. Sites were evaluated on the basis of eight factors:

- highway access (and visibility of Canon logo)
- vendor base
- number of Japanese firms in the area (Canon wanted to be the first)
- union status
- proximity to metro area and major airport
- labor availability
- proximity to seaport
- economic incentives offered at each location

Newport News was chosen from among the five sites.

D-SCAN, INC.

PROFILE OF THE U.S. COMPANY

HOME COUNTRIES OF PARENTS

Denmark and Switzerland

SIZE

A 76,000-square-foot facility is located on a 22-acre site.

PRODUCT

The plant fabricates modular, ready-to-assemble and assembled case goods furniture, of Scandinavian and contemporary designs.

PARENT COMPANIES

D-Scan, Inc. is a joint-venture company owned by Scanstyle Group, a multinational firm headquartered in Denmark, and by Diethelm & Co. of Zurich, Switzerland. Scanstyle Group was founded in 1968. The company designs, manufactures, and markets Scandinavian furniture. Scanstyle Group has 700 employees worldwide. The Diethelm Group was organized in 1871. This company engages in commodities trading, consumer marketing, surveying, construction, metals fabrication, management services, and furniture manufacture. The Diethelm Group has 3,000 employees. Diethelm & Co. is an international conglomerate with interests in textiles, commodities, and marketing of industrial and consumer products.

NUMBER OF EMPLOYEES

50 initially, increasing to 200

OPERATIONS

Teak veneer is imported from Burma, Indonesia, and Thailand. Some oak and other veneers are purchased in the United States. Metal hardware and fittings are brought in from Europe. Some shaped lumber pieces are shipped from sister plants in Singapore and Indonesia, and others are shaped in the United States. In the manufacturing process, the veneer is glued to locally produced particleboard. Gluing and shaping operations are performed with automated, computer-controlled equipment to form modular furniture components. Furniture is shipped both unassembled and assembled.

LOCATION AND COMMUNITY

South Boston, a community of 7,200 residents, is located 32 miles east of Danville and 10 miles north of the North Carolina state line. Traditionally, South Boston has been a trading center for the tobacco industry, but recent economic growth has occurred mostly in light industry and in timber-related businesses such as furniture and paper products.

D-SCAN — DECISION SEQUENCE

THE DECISION TO MANUFACTURE IN THE UNITED STATES

The United States is the largest market for Scandinavian teak furniture, and the management wanted to be closer to the U.S. market. To reduce transportation costs from its Southeast Asian plant and avoid import duties, management wanted a U.S. plant that could use locally produced materials, principally particleboard. This furniture line would complement imported models made in Southeast Asia.

Customer service, especially lead times on orders and product delivery schedules, would be improved from a U.S. facility.

Foreign-currency exchange rates made U.S. furniture manufacturing competitive relative to the plant in Singapore and European competitors.

SELECTION OF SPECIFIC GEOGRAPHIC REGIONS AND STATES

The management was originally predisposed toward a site in the High Point, N.C. area, the heart of the U.S. furniture industry.

The company found the High Point area too competitive for labor, especially for skilled craftsmen and foremen.

FINAL SITE SELECTION

Management began looking for sites farther and farther from High Point. Fifteen possible sites were found in North Carolina and Virginia.

The location in South Boston was chosen on the basis of the following factors:

- local and regional economic incentives
- availability of an ideal site in a South Boston industrial park — site of the proper size, with a railroad spur, good highway access, and a reasonable price
- very little competition for skilled labor
- adequate pool of unskilled laborers
- nearby supplies of particleboard from lumber companies
- proximity to the port of Hampton Roads
- constructive attitude of Virginia Governor Baliles and state officials
- superior performance by state, regional, and local economic development personnel

ERNI COMPONENTS
Division of Odin Components, Inc.
PROFILE OF THE U.S. COMPANY

HOME COUNTRIES OF PARENTS

West Germany and Switzerland

PRODUCT

The company manufactures DIN (Deutsche Industri Norm) connectors, which are pieces of equipment used to link or join electronic circuit boards.

NUMBER OF EMPLOYEES

45

OPERATIONS

The manufacturing operation involves the assembly of electronic components and other parts. Approximately 85 percent of the components are purchased from local suppliers. The proximity of local contact platers is important.

SIZE

The company leases a 16,400-square-foot factory.

PARENT COMPANIES

Originally a joint venture company, Odin Components, Inc., the U.S. parent of Erni Components, is now wholly owned by the West German company, Erni GmbH. Erni GmbH is, in turn, a subsidiary of Erni AG, which is based in Zurich, Switzerland.

LOCATION AND COMMUNITY

Richmond has been Virginia's capital for over 200 years and also served as the capital of the Confederacy. Located within a two-hour drive of both Washington, D.C., and the Atlantic coast, Richmond has become a major distribution, banking, and insurance center and the home of numerous corporate headquarters. The metropolitan area's total population is nearly 700,000, and recent economic growth has led to the restoration of the old tobacco and milling district into an area of boutiques and fine restaurants.

ERNI COMPONENTS — DECISION SEQUENCE

THE DECISION TO MANUFACTURE IN THE UNITED STATES

The management felt that customer service could be improved by manufacturing in the United States rather than by exporting from Europe. The cost-competitive nature of the business made customer service extremely important in the management's judgment.

The foreign-currency exchange rate had moved to a position that favored U.S. manufacture.

FINAL SITE SELECTION

Erni Components was initially a joint venture between Erni GmbH (West Germany) and Weidmuller (West Germany).

Weidmuller had an existing U.S. subsidiary with a plant in Chesterfield County, Virginia.

The executives of Erni's two parent companies decided to locate Erni in the same industrial park as the Weidmuller facility.

85

FIORUCCI FOODS CORPORATION

PROFILE OF THE U.S. COMPANY

HOME COUNTRY OF PARENT

Italy

PRODUCT

The company produces specialty meats, including prosciutto, sopressata, mortadella, coppa, salami, and pepperoni.

NUMBER OF EMPLOYEES

115

OPERATIONS

In Virginia, Fiorucci uses curing and aging methods pioneered by the company more than 130 years ago in Italy. The key difference between meats made in the traditional Italian way and those made by U.S. producers is this aging process, which for Fiorucci's prosciutto requires eight to fourteen months. The meats are aged naturally, without oven cooking to speed up the process. An exception is mortadella, which, by tradition, is oven-cooked slowly.

SIZE

Production facilities are located on a 200-acre site with a 100,000-square-foot factory. The initial investment was $20 million.

PARENT COMPANY

Cesare Fiorucci S.p.A. is Italy's largest meat manufacturer and, with $300 million in gross sales for 1987, the market leader in Europe. Employing more than 2,000 people at seven plants throughout Italy, Fiorucci distributes more than 600 different meat products in Italy, Germany, France, the United Kingdom, and the Netherlands, its primary markets. Fiorucci's distribution network in Italy includes approximately 40,000 clients. In its Parma, Italy, plant alone, 6,000 prosciutto hams are produced and distributed weekly.

The company is privately held and has been managed by the Fiorucci family for over 130 years.

LOCATION AND COMMUNITY

Colonial Heights is a thriving industrial community of 16,509 people approximately 20 miles south of Richmond. Major industries include metals and furniture.

FIORUCCI FOODS — DECISION SEQUENCE

THE DECISION TO MANUFACTURE IN THE UNITED STATES

The United States was perceived as a huge potential market for the company's specialty processed meats. Also, it was contemplated that exports could be made from a U.S. facility to Canada, Japan, and South America. Company products produced in Italy could not be exported to the United States because of a U.S. Department of Agriculture ban on all Italian meat imports.

SELECTION OF SPECIFIC GEOGRAPHIC REGIONS AND STATES

A member of the Fiorucci family was assigned the task of finding a site for the U.S. facility.

Four location factors were considered especially important:

- proximity to metropolitan markets in the Northeast and South
- a location near suppliers of pork and beef
- a state with right-to-work legislation
- a site in the most northerly region of the Southeast

The search was limited to Virginia and North Carolina.

FINAL SITE SELECTION

State economic development offices in both states were contacted, and several sites were examined.

A site in Colonial Heights near Richmond was chosen on the basis of the following judgments:

- The key manager had a favorable impression of Virginia and its business climate from prior business dealings in the state.
- The climate and geography in central Virginia are similar to the Parma region in Italy. These climatic conditions are favorable to the aging of proscuitto and other Fiorucci meats.
- The state and local economic development agencies put together an attractive package of site improvement in less than 30 days. The state provided an access road to the site, while the county arranged sewer and utility hookups.
- Interstate highway I-95 provided easy access to points north and south.
- Quality-of-life factors in the Richmond metropolitan area were perceived favorably:
  - Richmond is a metropolitan city with cinema, music, and other cultural amenities.
  - The East Coast location seemed closer to Italy.
  - The topography is similar to the Piedmont region of Italy.
- Richmond was perceived as having good airport connections.

FRANZ HAAS MACHINERY OF AMERICA, INC.

PROFILE OF THE U.S. COMPANY

HOME COUNTRY OF PARENT

Austria

SIZE

The company currently operates on a 63-acre site with a 21,000-square-foot factory. An expansion was planned for August, 1988.

PRODUCT

Products include machines and production plants for making wafer products. Franz Haas manufactures a complete range of small hand-operated units, semiautomatic plants, and fully automatic, computer-controlled production lines.

PARENT COMPANY

Franz Haas Waffelmaschinen GmbH is a privately held company based just outside Vienna. The company was established in 1901, and the Austrian company currently has around 600 employees. There are subsidiaries in West Germany, Brazil, and Hong Kong, as well as in the United States. Franz Haas has 60 percent of the world market for wafer/waffle-making equipment.

NUMBER OF EMPLOYEES

30

OPERATIONS

Machines are built to customers' specifications using an advanced computer-assisted design system. The factory is equipped with state-of-the-art machinery, most of which is computer-controlled.

LOCATION AND COMMUNITY

Richmond has been Virginia's capital for over 200 years and also served as the capital of the Confederacy. Located within a two-hour drive of both Washington, D.C., and the Atlantic coast, Richmond has become a major distribution, banking, and insurance center and the home of numerous corporate headquarters. The metropolitan area's total population is nearly 700,000, and recent economic growth has led to the restoration of the old tobacco and milling district into an area of boutiques and fine restaurants.

FRANZ HAAS — DECISION SEQUENCE

THE DECISION TO MANUFACTURE IN THE UNITED STATES

In 1980 the U.S. dollar was very low compared with the Austrian schilling. As a consequence, exporting products from Austria to the United States was expensive. A U.S. manufacturing plant was sought as a way to become more price competitive on machinery.

The management reasoned that a U.S. facility would lead to better customer service, especially maintenance, repairs, and on-site training of customer technicians.

SELECTION OF SPECIFIC GEOGRAPHIC REGIONS AND STATES

A large number of areas were originally considered, including the cities of Chicago and St. Louis and the regions of the Northeast, the Mid-Atlantic, and the Southeast.

The Virginia Department of Economic Development was contacted through its office in Brussels. Other state economic development agencies were also contacted.

FINAL SITE SELECTION

Virginia development officials flew company managers around the state to view prospective sites.

The final site selection analysis considered the following factors:

- proximity to major customers in the Northeast and Southeast
- proximity to a major deepwater port
- right-to-work legislation and low rates of unionization
- land costs of specific sites
- expected quality of life for Austrian employees

Richmond was determined to be the best site.

G. D PACKAGE MACHINERY INC.

PROFILE OF THE U.S. COMPANY

HOME COUNTRY OF PARENT

Italy

PRODUCT

The company assembles and services automatic wrapping machines which are used in the tobacco industry for the manufacture of cigarettes and cigarette packaging.

NUMBER OF EMPLOYEES

82

OPERATIONS

Machine parts and components are imported from Italy, assembled, and tested. In addition, the company handles the factory maintenance and repair of customer equipment, including tobacco machines for its customers in the United States.

SIZE

A 54,000-square-foot factory is located on a 12-acre site. The facility has been expanded three times in its 10-year history.

PARENT COMPANY

G. D S.p.A. is a privately owned company based in Bologna, Italy. The company manufactures confectionery, candy, and cigarette packaging or wrapping machines. Sales of tobacco machinery constitute 80 percent of the company's business. The company has plants for manufacturing components and assembling machines in Italy and Brazil. It has operations for machine assembly and customer service in West Germany, France, the United Kingdom, the United States, and Hong Kong.

LOCATION AND COMMUNITY

Richmond has been Virginia's capital for over 200 years and also served as the capital of the Confederacy. Located within a two-hour drive of both Washington, D.C., and the Atlantic coast, Richmond has become a major distribution, banking, and insurance center and the home of numerous corporate headquarters. The metropolitan area's total population is nearly 700,000, and recent economic growth has led to the restoration of the old tobacco and milling district into an area of boutiques and fine restaurants.

G. D PACKAGE MACHINERY — DECISION SEQUENCE

THE DECISION TO MANUFACTURE IN THE UNITED STATES

The company management wanted to provide better customer service by opening a U.S. assembly, repair, and parts center for its specialized machinery.

Richmond, Virginia was chosen as the site location principally because cigarette production is concentrated in the area.

$$\downarrow$$

FINAL SITE SELECTION

The management decided to locate in Richmond in order to provide better service to its major customer.

The staff of the large customer provided assistance in G. D Package Machinery's site search, including contacts with local realtors, land developers, and industrial park owners.

In 1977, the company found inexpensive office and warehouse space and opened a temporary, leased facility in Richmond.

In 1980, a permanent facility was constructed in Chesterfield County near Richmond.

HERMLE BLACK FOREST CLOCKS

PROFILE OF THE U.S. COMPANY

HOME COUNTRY OF PARENT

West Germany

PRODUCT

Quality clock movements are manufactured and sold to U.S. clock manufacturers.

NUMBER OF EMPLOYEES

70

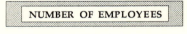

OPERATIONS

Clock movements are produced on an assembly line using both imported and domestically produced components. Modern operations techniques include efficient labor work stations that are either fully or semi-automated.

SIZE

The company operates in a 37,000-square-foot building on a 17-acre lot.

PARENT COMPANY

Franz Hermle & Sohn is a privately held company based in Gosheim, West Germany, with three plants in the home country.

Hermle sells wall, mantle, floor, ship's bell, and anniversary clocks with and without chimes. In addition, Hermle sells clock movements without cases worldwide.

LOCATION AND COMMUNITY

Amherst is located in Virginia's central Piedmont region, near both the James River and the Blue Ridge Mountains. With a population of 1,100, Amherst is just north of Lynchburg, one of the first industrial cities of the South. The area's diversified manufacturing base includes lumber products, furniture, textiles, and metal products.

HERMLE BLACK FOREST CLOCKS
DECISION SEQUENCE

THE DECISION TO MANUFACTURE IN THE UNITED STATES

The company management wanted to be closer to its U.S. customers to provide better service.

$\downarrow$

SELECTION OF SPECIFIC GEOGRAPHIC REGIONS AND STATES

The company management considered several states from the standpoint of:

- proximity to market
- the existence of right-to-work laws

The management contacted the Virginia Department of Economic Development in Brussels.

$\downarrow$

FINAL SITE SELECTION

Economic development officials put together a group of recommended sites. The sites were all visited.

The Amherst site was very appealing to the visitation group, met the search criteria, and was chosen.

INTERTAPE, INC.

PROFILE OF THE U.S. COMPANY

HOME COUNTRY OF PARENT

Canada

PRODUCT

Intertape, Inc., manufactures plastic film packaging tape for cartons and other uses.

NUMBER OF EMPLOYEES

60

OPERATIONS

In one process, the plant manufactures polypropylene film from plastic crystals. In other operations, wide sheets of film are coated with adhesive, wound into rolls, sliced into narrow rolls, and packaged for distribution.

SIZE

Manufacturing operations are conducted on a 70-acre site with a 90,000-square-foot factory. The original investment was $12 million.

PARENT COMPANY

Intertape Systems, Inc., is based in Montreal. Prior to the establishment of the U.S. facility, 80 percent of the Montreal output was exported to the United States.

LOCATION AND COMMUNITY

Located just north of the North Carolina border and 65 miles south of Lynchburg, Danville has a population of 44,900. In addition to being a world-famous tobacco marketing center, Danville has important textile and lumber industries as well.

INTERTAPE — DECISION SEQUENCE

THE DECISION TO MANUFACTURE IN THE UNITED STATES

Eighty percent of the sales of the Canadian parent company were made to U.S. customers.

Manufacturing in the United States would avoid a six percent tariff on exports from Canada.

Overall, the company needed new manufacturing capacity.

$\downarrow$

SELECTION OF SPECIFIC GEOGRAPHIC REGIONS AND STATES

Company executives contacted economic development officials in the Midwest, the Mid-Atlantic, and the Southeast.

Some states, including Pennsylvania, were eliminated because of heavy unionization.

Management decided to eliminate any site that was located more than one day's drive from the home office in Montreal.

A small town was preferred.

$\downarrow$

FINAL SITE SELECTION

The search was narrowed to Danville, Illinois, and Danville, Virginia.

Executives analyzed the two sites for:

- the availability of a building with a very special floor plan and dimensions
- the resourcefulness of local economic development agencies in meeting the company's special building requirements
- a work force with technical skills, high productivity, and a solid work ethic

Based on these factors, the management chose Danville, Virginia.

LINGUANOTO, INC.

PROFILE OF THE U.S. COMPANY

HOME COUNTRY OF PARENT

France

PRODUCT

The company manufactures contemporary upholstered office furniture.

NUMBER OF EMPLOYEES

5

OPERATIONS

The furniture is assembled in Richmond from components that are both imported and produced domestically. The company uses fabric from North Carolina, leather from New York, and plastic foam from Maryland.

SIZE

Linguanoto, Inc. has sales of approximately $1 million per year.

PARENT COMPANY

The parent company, Linguanoto S.A., is a privately owned company based in Paris. The company employs 350 with sales of roughly $25 million. In business for 55 years, the company has three manufacturing plants in France, specializing in upholstered chairs.

LOCATION AND COMMUNITY

Richmond has been Virginia's capital for over 200 years and also served as the capital of the Confederacy. Located within a two-hour drive of both Washington, D.C., and the Atlantic coast, Richmond has become a major distribution, banking, and insurance center and the home of numerous corporate headquarters. The metropolitan area's total population is nearly 700,000, and recent economic growth has led to the restoration of the old tobacco and milling district into an area of boutiques and fine restaurants.

LINGUANOTO — DECISION SEQUENCE

THE DECISION TO MANUFACTURE IN THE UNITED STATES

Management believed that assembling furniture in the United States from parts exported from France would be more cost-competitive than exporting finished furniture from France.

$\downarrow$

SELECTION OF SPECIFIC GEOGRAPHIC REGIONS AND STATES

Five location factors were important in the site selection analysis:

- An East Coast location was preferred. Management wanted to locate as close to Europe as possible.
- Management preferred a location near Washington, D.C., because it wanted to develop U.S. federal agencies as customers.
- The company needed a location near a deepwater port where furniture parts could be unloaded inexpensively.
- Labor costs were an important consideration in this labor-intensive business.
- The cost of insurance was also important.

$\downarrow$

FINAL SITE SELECTION

Based on these criteria, the company executives narrowed their search to possible locations in Richmond, Virginia. Baltimore, Maryland, was considered as a back-up location.

The management decided on one of the sites in Richmond.

NEW ALBERENE STONE CO.

PROFILE OF THE U.S. COMPANY

HOME COUNTRY OF PARENT

Finland

PRODUCT

The company manufactures soapstone fireplaces and stoves. Soapstone has unique heat-retention and heat-conducting qualities. It radiates heat more evenly and for longer periods than other materials do.

NUMBER OF EMPLOYEES

32

OPERATIONS

The factory is located at the only outcrop of soapstone in North America suitable for the company's needs. Mechanical saws making vertical and horizontal cuts are used to quarry stone blocks from the hillside. The stone blocks are placed beneath multi-blade gangsaws and cut into sheets one to five inches thick. Diamond surfacers smooth the stone sheets before they are cut into various sizes. Stones for fireplace applications are polished, edged, beveled, and drilled as necessary. The stones are then matched and assembled into fireplaces without the use of mortar. The stones are numbered, the fireplaces are disassembled, and the stones are stacked on pallets. Finally, the pallets are covered and banded for shipping.

SIZE

The company has 55,000 square feet of manufacturing space located on a 27-acre site.

PARENT COMPANY

Suomen Vuolukivi Oy (Finnish Soapstone Company) is a publicly held company in Nunnanlahti, Finland. New Alberene is one of five divisions reporting to the Finnish head office. The company made a public distribution of its stock in the Finnish over-the-counter market during 1988. The Vauhkonen family retains a majority ownership in the parent company.

LOCATION AND COMMUNITY

Schuyler is located 30 miles south of Charlottesville in a rural area of central Virginia near the foothills of the Blue Ridge Mountains. The region depends largely on agriculture for its economic livelihood.

NEW ALBERENE STONE — DECISION SEQUENCE

THE DECISION TO MANUFACTURE IN THE UNITED STATES

The market for New Alberene's Finnish soapstone stoves was growing in the United States.

Extremely high transportation costs on stoves exported from Finland and a U.S. import duty made U.S.-manufactured stoves cost-effective.

$\downarrow$

SELECTION OF SPECIFIC GEOGRAPHIC REGIONS AND STATES

Southern Albemarle County and Nelson County, Virginia have the highest quality soapstone usable for fireplaces in North America.

$\downarrow$

FINAL SITE SELECTION

Within the Albemarle/Nelson County quarry district, several shuttered quarries were abandoned and available. The management examined several facilities and chose one with the best existing buildings and equipment at a reasonable price.

OPTON, INC.

PROFILE OF THE U.S. COMPANY

HOME COUNTRY OF PARENT

Japan

PRODUCT

In Virginia, Opton, Inc., fabricates and chemically tempers glass for use in photocopiers.

NUMBER OF EMPLOYEES

30

OPERATIONS

Glass is purchased primarily from U.S. suppliers. The glass is lapped, polished, chemically tempered, and fabricated at the Virginia facility. The company is considering an expansion of its product line to include glass with other photocopier components attached.

SIZE

The company leases a 60,000-square-foot factory on a 4 1/2-acre site.

PARENT COMPANY

In Japan, Tatsuguchi Kougyo Glass Co. Ltd. produces glass for:

— copiers
— telefacsimile machines
— clocks and watches

Tatsuguchi Kougyo has more than 100 employees in Japan.

LOCATION AND COMMUNITY

Newport News, with a population of 157,100, is located at the mouth of the James River on the north side of Hampton Roads, the nation's largest natural harbor. The city's economy is based on shipbuilding and repair, manufacturing, seafood, and tourism.

OPTON — DECISION SEQUENCE

THE DECISION TO MANUFACTURE IN THE UNITED STATES

In Japan, Canon (the copier maker) is Opton's largest customer. When Canon opened its manufacturing facility in Newport News, Virginia, Opton decided to maintain its good relationship with Canon by setting up a manufacturing plant nearby.

Company executives wanted to use a new plant to expand and diversify Opton's customer base in the United States, using the Canon business as a solid base on which to build.

FINAL SITE SELECTION

Opton executives decided to locate near Canon, in or near Newport News.

Management at Opton contacted the Tokyo office of Virginia's Department of Economic Development. The management was referred to the Department's office in Richmond. Officials there put Opton managers in touch with economic development officials in Newport News.

Because of time constraints, which called for the quickest possible start-up schedule, the Opton management showed a preference for buildings that were already constructed and available.

Newport News economic development officials showed Opton executives various locations near the Canon plant.

A shell building with suitable specifications was found in a local industrial park. The Opton managers purchased the building and made interior modifications.

SAN-J INTERNATIONAL

PROFILE OF THE U.S. COMPANY

HOME COUNTRY OF PARENT

Japan

PRODUCT

San-J International makes tamari soy sauce and other products from fermented soy beans. Whereas most soy sauce contains wheat, tamari does not. Soy, salt, and water are ingredients of both products. Soy products are made for the retail market (supermarkets and health food stores) and for the wholesale market (major food corporations).

NUMBER OF EMPLOYEES

22, growing to 35 at full capacity

OPERATIONS

Rail carloads of whole soybeans, soy meal, and wheat are shipped in from grain-growing regions of the United States. The soy is cooked, soaked in water, then inoculated with bacteria to induce fermentation. After the addition of salt and more water, the mixture is allowed to ferment in storage for several months. The mixture is then pressed through cloth filters to extract the tamari, or soy sauce liquids. The liquids are pasteurized, filtered, and packaged in small glass bottles or 55-gallon drums.

SIZE

The U.S. company operates in a 44,000-square-foot building, with 9.5 acres of land. Sales are approximately $5 million.

PARENT COMPANY

San-J International is a wholly owned subsidiary of San-Jirushi Corp., a Japanese foods corporation. San-Jirushi Corp., founded in 1804, has been managed by seven generations of the Sato family. Tamari and soy sauce, miso (a soy paste), and oriental-style sauces are made in Japan by San-Jirushi. Its home city, Kuwana, is a traditional home of tamari.

The company controls about 60 percent of the Japanese tamari market plus most of the growing U.S. market.

LOCATION AND COMMUNITY

Richmond has been Virginia's capital for over 200 years and also served as the capital of the Confederacy. Located within a two-hour drive of both Washington, D.C., and the Atlantic coast, Richmond has become a major distribution, banking, and insurance center and the home of numerous corporate headquarters. The metropolitan area's total population is nearly 700,000, and recent economic growth has led to the restoration of the old tobacco and milling district into an area of boutiques and fine restaurants.

SAN-J INTERNATIONAL — DECISION SEQUENCE

THE DECISION TO MANUFACTURE IN THE UNITED STATES

The Japanese market for soy-based products was mature. Prospects for future growth were much greater in the United States.

By 1985 the foreign currency exchange rate between the dollar and the yen made U.S. production cost-effective.

SELECTION OF SPECIFIC GEOGRAPHIC REGIONS AND STATES

Special climatic needs for the fermentation of soy products dictated a location in an area with high humidity and high summer temperatures. Management preferred locations on or near the coast to duplicate the climatic conditions at the home plant in Japan.

Company executives originally considered the states of California, Oregon, Maryland, and Virginia.

California and Oregon were eliminated because of high land and labor costs.

The company was involved in a joint venture for the sales and distribution of its products in the United States. The minority joint venture partner lived near Richmond, Virginia, and favored a location near his home and office.

In addition to the personal preferences of the joint venture partner, Virginia was favored for the following reasons:

- a location close to major food processors that use soy products
- right-to-work laws and low unionization
- a climate favorable to soy products' fermentation
- a long, noteworthy history, or "Virginia mystique," that appealed to the family members of the 180-year-old parent company in Japan

The management opened a sales and administrative office near Richmond while the search for a manufacturing location was conducted.

FINAL SITE SELECTION

After the management decided to find a location near Richmond, it contacted Virginia's Department of Economic Development and the local economic development agency for Henrico County.

Company executives looked at several sites, taking into account:

- low land costs
- service by a railroad spur

A suitable site was found in a Richmond-area industrial park.

SUMITOMO MACHINERY CORPORATION OF AMERICA

PROFILE OF THE U.S. COMPANY

HOME COUNTRY OF PARENT

Japan

PRODUCT

The plant produces cyclo speed reducers, which are power-transmission components of industrial machinery.

NUMBER OF EMPLOYEES

140 at plant start-up in July, 1988. Employment will eventually reach 500.

OPERATIONS

The plant houses numerous machines which produce finished components from basic castings, forgings, and bar stock (raw materials). These components are for shipment elsewhere in North America or for use as completed speed reducers and gear motors. Specialty machining work is also done within the new facility.

SIZE

The manufacturing facility will initially be 150,000 square feet, expanding to 500,000 square feet.

PARENT COMPANY

Sumitomo Heavy Industries, based in Tokyo, has nearly 10,000 employees and annual sales of $2 billion. Its principal products are power-plant components, industrial machinery, engines, ships, and offshore oil-drilling platforms. Through interlocking share holdings, it is part of the Sumitomo Group, which traces its origins to the late sixteenth century.

The company started its U.S. operations in the early 1960s when a facility was opened in New Jersey to assemble finished products from components exported from Japan. Sumitomo Machinery Corporation of America now has six facilities throughout North America, employing 200 people.

LOCATION AND COMMUNITY

Chesapeake, with a 340-square-mile area, is the second largest incorporated city in Virginia. Chesapeake has a population of 130,000. The Elizabeth River, which runs through the city into the harbor of Hampton Roads, is the site of many chemical and industrial facilities.

SUMITOMO MACHINERY— DECISION SEQUENCE

THE DECISION TO MANUFACTURE IN THE UNITED STATES

The company had been assembling products and conducting sales and distribution operations since the 1960s.

By 1985 the U.S. dollar had declined relative to the yen to the point that manufacture in the United States became feasible. The company decided to manufacture certain products that had previously been exported from Japan.

$\downarrow$

SELECTION OF SPECIFIC GEOGRAPHIC REGIONS AND STATES

Company executives focused on ten Southern states where right-to-work legislation had been enacted.

$\downarrow$

FINAL SITE SELECTION

The management analyzed locations in the ten states based upon six primary factors:

- deepwater port
- a location that was centralized relative to its major marketing area — the eastern half of the country
- a large pool of semi-skilled workers
- the helpfulness of state and local government and economic development agencies
- land costs (which, because they were so similar between locations, ceased to be important in the comparison)
- economic incentives (which, for the same reason as land costs, ceased to be important)

Based on these criteria, the management chose a site in Chesapeake, Virginia.

VDO – YAZAKI CORPORATION
PROFILE OF THE U.S. COMPANY

West Germany and Japan

VDO-Yazaki makes electrical instruments and gauges for the automobile, farm implement, marine, and aviation industries. Products include unattached gauges and complete instrument panels mounted and ready for installation in automobile interiors.

380

Raw materials and components are assembled into finished electrical units using both hand assembly and computer-aided robotic assembly.

The company's manufacturing operations are conducted at a 180,000-square-foot facility on a 20-acre site.

VDO-Yazaki is a joint venture between VDO Adolf Schindling, AG and Yazaki Corporation. Both joint venture firms are equally represented on the board of directors.

Adolf Schindling, with 20,000 employees worldwide, is the world's largest independent gauge and automobile instrument manufacturer. Headquartered in Schwalback/Raunus, West Germany, its annual sales are approximately $550 million.

Yazaki Corporation manufactures industrial wires, cables, and wire harnesses for use in automobile electrical systems. Headquar-tered in Tokyo, Yazaki has subsidiaries on four continents and employs 19,200 people. The company was founded in 1941, and it is managed by members of the Yazaki family.

Winchester, a city of 21,000, is situated at the northern end of the Shenandoah River Valley within a few miles of West Virginia, Maryland, and Pennsylvania. A transportation crossroads since colonial times, the city is home to many large manufacturing facilities and is a center for agricultural and fruit production.

VDO – YAZAKI — DECISION SEQUENCE

THE DECISION TO MANUFACTURE IN THE UNITED STATES

Volkswagen was a major VDO customer in West Germany. After Volkswagen built a plant in Pennsylvania, VDO decided to build a U.S. facility to extend its supplier relationship into the United States.

Using Volkswagen as a major customer — one whose business justified building a U.S. plant — the company intended to expand its U.S. business to other customers.

Products made in the United States were cost-competitive with those exported from Germany, and the U.S. plant could provide improvements in customer service.

$\downarrow$

SELECTION OF SPECIFIC GEOGRAPHIC REGIONS AND STATES

Company executives looked for a site with six characteristics:

- a location within 500 miles of both the Pennsylvania Volkswagen plant and other major automobile plants, mostly centered around the Great Lakes
- access to a deepwater port
- interstate highways and railroad connections
- an inland location, away from the corrosive salts contained in sea air
- right-to-work legislation
- economic incentives, including financing

The management originally considered Pennsylvania, Maryland, Virginia, West Virginia, and North Carolina.

The various states offered fairly comparable economic incentive packages.

In management's judgment, the other five factors favored Virginia.

$\downarrow$

FINAL SITE SELECTION

Management contacted Virginia's Department of Economic Development.

State officials, in conjunction with local economic development agencies, selected several promising sites. These sites were then toured with company officials in the governor's airplane.

The site in Winchester satisfied the company's criteria better than the other sites.

VSL CORPORATION

PROFILE OF THE U.S. COMPANY

Switzerland

The sales volume of VSL Eastern is $40 million, with total U.S. sales of $65 million. The company rents 30,000 square feet in Springfield, Virginia.

VSL manufactures post-tensioned concrete systems for use in the construction of highways and in buildings. The company also offers services for the complete design and construction of turnkey construction projects.

VSL is a subsidiary of Losinger, Ltd., an engineering and construction firm headquartered in Berne, Switzerland. Losinger is a major international construction company with subsidiaries, affiliates, and licensees in over 30 countries on six continents. Originally, all U.S. operations were managed from the company's California office. In 1985 U.S. operations were segregated into two divisions, East and West. The eastern headquarters was established in Virginia. Both U.S. divisions report directly to Switzerland.

VSL Eastern Total — 242
Virginia — 63

Springfield is part of the rapidly growing northern Virginia suburban areas of Washington, D.C. In recent years, rapid growth of its own high technology and defense firms has transformed it from a suburb of commuters to an employment area.

Company designs, engineers, and constructs complete post-tensioned concrete systems. It also manufactures extruded steel cables which are fabricated to meet engineering requirements.

VSL CORPORATION — DECISION SEQUENCE

THE DECISION TO MANUFACTURE IN THE UNITED STATES

The company had operated a subsidiary in California since 1966 to design, manufacture, and install commercial structures using concrete reinforced with post-tensioned steel.

In 1972 a sales office was opened in the Springfield, Virginia area to service the eastern United States.

Because VSL's products are very expensive to transport across the country, management decided to set up an eastern U.S. facility to produce post-tensioning and earth-retaining concrete products.

SELECTION OF SPECIFIC GEOGRAPHIC REGIONS AND STATES

Management wanted a location in the East near major eastern construction projects.

Proximity to a port was necessary for the importation of reinforcing steel strands.

FINAL SITE SELECTION

A major VSL competitor set up a facility in northern Virginia. VSL wanted to locate near this competitor to avoid being at a disadvantage from a customer-service perspective.

The company chose Springfield, Virginia for three major reasons:

- close to the existing headquarters of VSL Eastern
- close to major competitor
- close to the ports of Baltimore, Maryland, and Norfolk, Virginia

WALTER GRINDERS

PROFILE OF THE U.S. COMPANY

HOME COUNTRY OF PARENT

West Germany

PRODUCT

The company manufactures computer-controlled machines for grinding metal.

NUMBER OF EMPLOYEES

115

OPERATIONS

Initially, when Walter Grinders established its operations in Virginia, the company assembled components shipped from West Germany. Now the company manufactures some components on-site and buys others from U.S. suppliers, to supplement its imports from abroad. In addition, some machine design work is now done in the United States.

SIZE

The company owns a 26,000-square-foot plant situated on 3 acres. The U.S. company has sales in the $12 million to $15 million range.

PARENT COMPANY

Walter Grinders is owned by Montanwerke Walter GmbH headquartered in Tubingen, West Germany. Walter GmbH is an international company specializing in the field of tungsten carbides and tungsten carbide cutting tools, as well as computerized numerically controlled (CNC) grinders. Walter companies are located in five European countries in addition to Germany. Consolidated sales are about $120 million.

LOCATION AND COMMUNITY

A community of 19,000, Fredericksburg is located 55 miles south of Washington, D.C. Its traditional economy, based on light industry, is being changed dramatically by the economic growth generated by Washington, D.C. The city is experiencing rapid development of subdivisions and shopping centers, and a growing number of its citizens commute daily to Washington.

WALTER GRINDERS — DECISION SEQUENCE

THE DECISION TO MANUFACTURE IN THE UNITED STATES

The company had been exporting to the United States for many years. Sales, however, had not increased in accordance with management's assessment of the market potential.

A U.S. plant would provide the facilities and the technical support to upgrade customer service in three ways:

- better design and installation service
- faster and more effective repair and maintenance services
- better training of customer technical personnel

SELECTION OF SPECIFIC GEOGRAPHIC REGIONS AND STATES

The management originally considered the Midwest and the Southeast.

Specifically, the list of states included Illinois, Indiana, Virginia, North Carolina, and South Carolina.

Management contacted the state economic development agencies in these states.

FINAL SITE SELECTION

The following criteria were important in the location analysis:

- right-to-work legislation and unionization levels
- proximity to international airports
- quality-of-life factors such as climate and life-style
- the overall economic growth and business climate of each area
- the perceived work ethic of employees

Of sites shown in various states, management preferred Spotsylvania County, Virginia for these reasons:

- low personal property tax rates in comparison with rates in a nearby community
- nearby access to Chesapeake Bay for recreation

WEIDMULLER INC.

PROFILE OF THE U.S. COMPANY

West Germany

Products manufactured in Virginia include terminal blocks and connectors for electronic circuit boards.

76

The production process is largely an assembly operation of parts and components. Most of the components are imported from West Germany. Some plastics components are, however, injection-molded in Richmond.

The company operates in a 26,000-square-foot plant located on a 21-acre site.

C.A. Weidmuller GmbH is a privately held family company located in Detmold, West Germany. C. A. Weidmuller has nine production plants among 22 marketing operations serving 15 countries. The parent company offers a comprehensive range of electrical and electronic connection systems for the power generation, distribution, and control markets. The worldwide sales of Weidmuller are around 600 million DM (approximately $276 million). Weidmuller Inc. is one of four C. A. Weidmuller GmbH subsidiaries in the United States.

Richmond has been Virginia's capital for over 200 years and also served as the capital of the Confederacy. Located within a two-hour drive of both Washington, D.C., and the Atlantic coast, Richmond has become a major distribution, banking, and insurance center and the home of numerous corporate headquarters. The metropolitan area's total population is nearly 700,000, and recent economic growth has led to the restoration of the old tobacco and milling district into an area of boutiques and fine restaurants.

WEIDMULLER — DECISION SEQUENCE

THE DECISION TO MANUFACTURE IN THE UNITED STATES

Previously the company had exported into the United States from West Germany, using a manufacturer's representative agency to handle sales and distribution functions.

Arrangements with the agency, however, were not deemed satisfactory. The Weidmuller management wanted to set up its own sales and marketing capability to exploit the growing U.S. market, particularly since the German market was saturated.

After concluding that U.S. manufacture would be cost-competitive, management decided to build a complete manufacturing, marketing, and distribution capability in the United States.

$\downarrow$

SELECTION OF SPECIFIC GEOGRAPHIC REGIONS AND STATES

The management originally considered the cities of Richmond, Virginia; Atlanta, Georgia; and Houston, Texas.

The choice was narrowed to an East Coast location.

Proximity to a deepwater port was important.

$\downarrow$

FINAL SITE SELECTION

After evaluating the possible sites, management decided to locate in Chesterfield County near Richmond.

PART 5

SUMMARY AND CONCLUSIONS

New insights about the strategic thinking and decision-making processes of foreign direct investors are provided in this study. The findings are based on interviews and subsequent follow-up with executives in the U.S. affiliates of 20 foreign companies. Each of these companies had made a recent manufacturing investment in the United States. Enhanced understanding of the role of management in FDI and plant-location decisions was the primary focus of the research. Such an understanding was intended to be of help to other foreign companies considering U.S. investments and to people or organizations in this country with an interest in attracting such investments.

The desire to accomplish certain strategic objectives is instrumental in the decision to invest in the United States. All but one of the 20 companies had been exporting products to the U.S. market from their home countries. In these export operations, difficulties with customer service were being encountered, largely because of the great distances between U.S. customers and foreign sources, and the companies were incurring operating and transportation costs above those anticipated for a U.S. manufacturing operation. A desire to overcome these disadvantages and to accomplish other market, cost, and profit objectives were key factors in the decision process.

Eighteen of the 20 investment decisions were heavily conditioned by market considerations. In four of the eighteen market-driven decisions, cost reasons were also compelling. Two types of market strategies dominated management thinking about new U.S. plants. First, the companies wanted to concentrate their investments in markets of substantial size with favorable growth characteristics and political stability, for which the U.S. market was ideal. Second, within such a market, customer service objectives were significant. A U.S. manufacturing and operating base could reduce lead times for manufacturing and delivery, upgrade technical service, improve customer relations on inquiries and complaints, and foster more frequent direct contact with customers.

Six of the 20 decisions were strongly driven by strategies relating to cost reduction. Transportation costs were mentioned most frequently. Raw material costs, import duties, and compensation costs were also cited. Favorable foreign currency exchange rates influenced the timing of seven decisions. In four of the six companies where cost objectives were extremely important, the attainment of market objectives was likewise significant.

The investments were guided by other strategies as well. As one example, several companies mentioned a "global strategy," in which different international markets are served by local plants — the North American market being served by a new U.S. facility. In another example, the U.S. investments were made to meet certain profitability and return–on–investment objectives. Finally, several executives mentioned a basic, long–term psychological commitment to the U.S. market. It was important for them to be in this market with "both feet," even if that entailed some short–term costs.

Certain market and cost strategies that were important in the investment decisions continued to be significant after the plants began operation. Examples are customer service, cost-effectiveness, and profitability goals. A study of the ongoing operations after plant start-ups, however, also brought to light other important strategies in these foreign companies. Objectives concerning cost effectiveness and product quality were obviously important. The plants were modern and used state–of–the–art technology. The facilities had excellent materials–handling equipment, and the operations appeared to be labor-efficient. Sophisticated computer–controlled processing equipment was in place in at least half the plants.

The prevailing management philosophy governing the foreign affiliates was one of decentralization. Except for controls over capital expenditure programs and some high–level recruitment and compensation decisions, there was considerable delegation of authority from abroad. The local managers were proud of their autonomy.

Most of the companies relied on nationals from their parent companies to oversee their U.S. investments. The chief executive officers in 17 of the 20 companies were foreign nationals. The total number of managerial personnel on assignment to the U.S. affiliate from abroad seldom exceeded two, although four managers in one company and five in another were foreign. One company had 35 foreign nationals in technical assignments, but the number did not exceed four in the remaining companies. The U.S. immigration laws and regulations limit the number of foreign nationals, and the stringency of U.S. immigration measures is a major irritant for executives in these companies.

Every company had a policy of being fully competitive on wage and salary levels. To avoid a possible disruption of local wage patterns, managers were concerned that they not overpay to attract critically needed skills. Most executives also exhibited a strong interest in being completely competitive on employee benefit programs. All plants were nonunionized, and the managers wanted to continue operations without collective bargaining units.

Executives in the foreign affiliates also wanted their corporations be recognized as good citizens in their adopted country. Such concerns prompted enlightened attitudes and positive actions on matters pertaining to the well–being of employees, community relations, and environmental concerns.

"Buy American" policies or concerns for sourcing existed in most companies. However, over half of the companies still relied heavily on foreign sources for materials, components, and supplies — often importing semi–finished goods from their own plants. Most executives intended to increase their purchases from U.S. suppliers, with a stated intermediate goal of making 50 percent or more of their purchases locally.

Our research into the 20 plant–location decisions sheds considerable light on the managerial process involved in such activities. After the decision to manufacture in the United States has been made, the site selection process in most companies involves three stages — the selection of a specific geographic region in the United States, the selection of states within that region, and the final decision on a specific site in a particular community. Our research was confined to plant start-ups, not mergers and acquisitions. A somewhat different series of actions characterizes the plant-location process in merger and acquisition situations.

For each stage in the selection process, the managements established location criteria, such as nearness to markets and adequate labor availability. Regions, states, and particular sites are measured against these criteria. The managerial judgments at each stage are based upon a mixture of intuition, preconceptions, personal interests, and careful analysis.

After making the decision to establish manufacturing operations in the United States, 15 of the 20 companies selected geographic regions at a distinct stage in the selection process. Special circumstances led five of the companies to move immediately to particular localities.

Our research indicates that executives of foreign companies often have fairly strong insights or preferences about one or more particular geographic regions, even before the site selection process begins. The Southeast, for example, has a reputation for a moderate cost of living, generally harmonious labor relations, a good employee work ethic, excellent seaports, and favorable quality–of–life attributes. There are negative perceptions about the availability of selected employee skills, general levels of education, and air transportation convenience.

In only a few cases were the significant attributes of one region, such as land costs, taxes, or labor rates, compared carefully with such attributes in other regions. Conclusions on these matters were based instead on an informal body of knowledge acquired by the foreign executives through travel, discussion with other executives, and media exposure.

After one or more regions were selected, most companies limited their location search to two or three states from these regions. The reasons for choosing one state over another are somewhat obscure, however. We did not observe a great deal of rigorous state–by–state analysis of location factors in the state selection process, although a high degree of economic vitality in a state was clearly a significant factor. Marketing efforts of state economic development officials located in foreign offices were influential in some cases. Many of the criteria for selecting states were the same as those for selecting specific regions, but more selectivity could be exercised in choosing a state. For example, being close to markets or seaports could be objectives in both cases, but some states in a region are closer to markets or seaports than others.

After two or three states were chosen, the search for a specific site began. Most companies contacted state economic development agencies for help at this point. State officials, using the criteria supplied by the companies, drew up a list of four or more specific sites. These site–specific criteria included acreage needs, building size and layout requirements, interstate highway access, utility specifications, and desired community characteristics. Suggested sites were ordinarily in different communities.

The sites and the communities in which they are located were evaluated by executives on plant tours arranged by state economic development officials. Two or three days were normally required to complete the visits in Virginia. In each community on the tour, the visiting delegation would generally be joined by local economic development officials and frequently by members of the business community. Negotiations regarding zoning, possible economic support from the community, building design permits, access roads, and similar matters were usually resolved at a local level. In addition to site recommendations and site tours, state officials were sometimes asked to prepare detailed site analyses. Attributes of a site such as tax rates or wage levels were then compared with those in another location, often in a different state.

Few of the companies purchased sites with established buildings on them. Most companies in our study decided on locations in industrial parks where new buildings were constructed to specifications.

Identification and analysis of the site selection factors important to foreign managers is a significant result of this study. In open-ended interviews, we asked executives to identify factors that were either "very important" or "moderately important" in their decisions. Nineteen different location factors were mentioned, although not always identifiable with specific stages of the process (regional, state, site, and community selection.

Finding a location close to U.S. markets and customers was an extremely important factor. As foreign exporters to the United States, these companies were at an inherent disadvantage because of cultural, language, tariff, and distance barriers.

Right–to–work laws were identified as highly significant in attracting companies to Virginia and the Southeast, although detailed discussion with executives led us to believe that the low level of unionization in Virginia was the real attraction. Many of the executives seemed to use the terms *right–to–work, low unionization,* and *labor climate* almost interchangeably. There was a strong preference for nonunion environments. On the other hand, several executives pointed out that their companies had other operations that were unionized, and they were prepared to operate here with unions if necessary.

The role played by state economic development agencies was a key factor in the site selection process. Economic development officials are viewed as highly professional and enthusiastic. They make the executives feel comfortable about the State and community decisions. In fact, several executives stated outright that the dedication and professionalism of state and local officials were critical in their choice of a Virginia location.

Ready access to a deepwater seaport was critical for some companies which import significant amounts of raw materials, components, and subassemblies. Most of these companies restricted their search to sites located within a 100-mile radius of a seaport. For them, the Hampton Roads (Norfolk) and Baltimore ports were both attractive.

The cost of land was a fairly significant consideration. Thus, comparatively attractive land costs in the Southeast contributed to the appeal of this region. Land costs became a compelling factor for a few companies when a choice was made between alternate tracts in a particular community. Most companies constructed their buildings to specifications; therefore, cost of buildings was not a location issue. Although construction cost levels were not a major location factor, southeastern construction costs were perceived as comparatively low.

Quality–of–life factors — the positive or negative impact of a community, state, or region on the personal lives of employees — were important. Therefore, the companies considered such matters as climate, educational facilities and opportunities, cultural appeal, recreational potential, attractiveness of local neighborhoods, and local transportation convenience.

Some companies were influenced by economic incentives offered by local communities or the state. Incentives included financing assistance through the use of industrial revenue bonds, industrial training provided by a State organization, recruitment screening by another state agency, and the construction of access roads. No direct monetary grants or tax forgiveness was involved in any situation. Overall, economic incentives did not appear to play a *decisive* role in any of the 20 decisions.

Accessibility and quality of air, rail, or highway transportation were important location factors. The ability to make direct flights to points in the United States and abroad was viewed as important; yet executives in the 20 companies made decisions to locate throughout Virginia despite the nonavailability of such flights outside of the Washington area. In the selection of sites, several companies needed railroad sidings, and one insisted on a location near the intersection of east-west and north-south interstate highways. Most executives found the highway system generally acceptable at more than one location.

Sites close to raw material sources were attractive in some cases. One company quarried soapstone to manufacture specialty stoves, one processed meats from the area, and a furniture manufacturer drew from local supplies of lumber. The availability of nearby raw material supplies was also "moderately important" to a chemical company and to a second furniture manufacturer.

The available labor pool in an area, along with the skills and attitudes of employees in the pool, was important. Executives in these companies were seeking an ample pool of unskilled labor, an existing cadre of trained employees, and workers possessing a "good work ethic" and constructive attitudes. After the plant decisions were made, expectations regarding employees were not always realized. Several companies had to implement unplanned training programs, and executives in two companies were disappointed with the work habits and motivation of employees.

A number of miscellaneous factors were cited. Executives in four European companies limited their search to Atlantic coast locations, because they wanted to be as close to Europe as possible, thereby reducing travel, cutting down on communication and relocation costs, and minimizing the sense of separation from home. Some companies conducted their search with specific climatic conditions in mind. Particular temperature and humidity conditions were significant in three situations — in two for the aging of foods and in one for the growing of grapes. An environment free from airborne corrosive salts was important in another. In two joint venture companies, the desire to find a site near the plant of a parent company narrowed the search. In two companies that already had other U.S. plant operations, the prior existence of these facilities was a key factor in determining the location of the new plant. For two other companies, the existence of a "favorable" business climate was a fairly important consideration. Executives in one European and one Japanese company were impressed with the cultural heritage and history of Virginia. To enhance their own market visibility, executives in two other companies were interested in finding locations near significant competitors. Favorable wage rates were an influential factor in one location decision. Finally, executives in a chemical company sought a plant location that was distant from residential housing.

Certain conclusions can be drawn from our research findings. The reasons for foreign direct investments in the United States as reported in this study are consistent with the findings of other researchers. The size and attractiveness of the U.S. market is an important theme in this and previous studies. Cost factors are important common considerations, but in terms of emphasis, one difference in this study may be the prominence attached to "customer service" and "nearness to markets" as market–oriented reasons for investment.

Our finding that companies approach the plant–location decision as a multi-stage process also reinforces earlier research findings. Previous research, however, described the decision process as a two-stage process involving (1) the selection of a region or a group of states and (2) the choice of specific communities or sites. We found, however, that three stages are ordinarily involved in the decision process — (1) the selection of a region, (2) the selection of specific states in that region, and (3) the choice of specific communities or sites.

With regard specifically to plant–location factors, there are two fairly important differences between our findings and those of other studies. Our research highlights the important role played by state and local economic development agencies in influencing the decision. Wage levels, on the other hand, were found to be less important as a consideration in our study than they have been in many others. Nearness to markets, labor union prospects, and proximity to seaports were important factors found in this and in other research.

APPENDIX:
FOREIGN DIRECT INVESTMENT
TRENDS

The past decade has been characterized by significant increases in the number and magnitude of foreign direct investments in the United States, and the 20 investments considered in this study took place within the context of these broad trends. There are four major reasons for the growth of FDI activity in the United States in recent years. First, business enterprises in other countries, particularly in Western Europe and the Pacific Rim, have found growth rates for their products falling off as demand has matured. As a consequence, they have turned to the United States, the largest unified market in the world, as a source of future growth. Second, the comparative political and social stability of the United States has made it a "safe haven" for investments by foreigners. Third, the recent wave of takeovers, restructurings, and divestitures by U.S. corporations has provided opportunities for foreign ownership. Finally, the exchange rate between the dollar and other major currencies has been favorable to FDI during some, but not all, recent periods.

GROWTH IN FOREIGN INVESTMENT

The total investment by foreign companies in all industries in the United States, as reported by the Department of Commerce, grew continuously from 1977 to 1986, the last year for which data are available. The Department of Commerce provides information for the following industry sectors: mining, petroleum, manufacturing, wholesale trade, retail trade, banking, finance (other than banking), real estate, and other industries such as agriculture, forestry and fishing, construction, trucking, communication and public utilities, and services. The Department of Commerce defines foreign affiliate as any company in the United States that is 10 percent or more owned by a foreign company. The Department reports gross book value in plant, property, and equipment, net book value, and capital additions for foreign affiliates in the United States.

In this appendix, an analysis is presented of the data on gross book value and capital additions. (We examined growth in net book value as well as increases in gross book value, but the growth patterns between the two were so similar that we decided to report only gross book value and capital additions.) Gross book value is a measure of the cumulative investments in the industries before depreciation, depletion, and similar charges. The figures have been adjusted for retirements and property sales. For simplicity, gross book value of plant, property, and equipment is referred to simply as "gross investment." Capital additions to gross investments include capital expenditures for plant, property, and equipment and the costs of corporate acquisitions.

As shown in Table A.1, the total gross investment of foreign affiliates in all industries in the United States grew from $66.8 billion in 1977 to $317.6 billion in 1986, an annual increase of 18.9 percent (shown on Table A.1 as growth during the nine years from 1978 through 1986). These gross investment figures are in nominal dollars; they reflect the impact of inflation changes that altered the value of the U.S. dollar. On the basis of inflation-adjusted (or constant-value) dollars, the total gross investment in all industries grew at a 15.0 percent annual rate between 1977 and 1986. The comparable annual growth rate for foreign affiliates in the manufacturing sector alone was similar, 14.8 percent. The gross investment in manufacturing industries was $113.0 billion in 1986, 35.6 percent of the $317.6 billion in all industries.

In Virginia, the total gross investment of foreign affiliates grew at a much greater rate than the national average. The gross investment in the state for foreign affiliates in all industries increased from $824 million in 1977 to $5.5 billion in 1986 , an annual growth rate of 23.6 percent. The growth rate in constant dollars was somewhat lower, 19.5 percent. The gross investment for Virginia affiliates engaged in manufacturing industries grew at a somewhat greater annual rate, 21.9 percent.

Figure A.1 shows growth rates of gross investments in nominal dollars for the nine-year period, 1978 through 1986, and for three-year periods — 1978 through 1980, 1981 through 1983, and 1984 through 1986. Growth rates are shown for all industries and for manufacturing industries. Data for three areas are given: the United States as a whole, the Southeast Atlantic region composed of Maryland, Virginia, North Carolina, South Carolina and Georgia, and the state of Virginia. Figure A.2 presents growth rates for the same periods for gross investments that have been converted to constant dollars to eliminate inflationary effects.

As shown in Figure A.2, the growth rates of foreign affiliates in Virginia during the 1981–1983 period exceeded those in the other periods, both for all industries and for manufacturing industries alone. There was substantial growth of Virginia foreign affiliates engaged in manufacturing during this period: assets grew at a 47.9 percent annual rate. The comparable annual growth rates of manufacturing affiliates were 19.4 percent for the United States and 15.8 percent for the Southeast Atlantic region (specific growth rates shown on Table A.1).

The most recent three–year period shown, 1984–1986, was marked by much lower growth rates for gross investment than the 1981–1983 period. Not incidentally, during much of the later period, the value of the U.S. dollar was high relative to the Japanese yen and most European currencies. Thus, foreigners wishing to invest in the United States during this period found investments more costly than in the previous periods.

Table A.1 shows that different industries in Virginia have experienced widely divergent growth rates in gross investment. Note, as one illustration, that the chemicals and allied products industry grew at a 15.5 percent annual rate during the 1984–1986 period, while the food and kindred products segment reported a 7.3 percent annual decline in growth.

Growth rates were also erratic over time within any one industry; particular industries experienced radically different growth from period to period. For example, growth in gross investments in chemicals and allied products was substantial from 1980 to 1983, increasing from $270 million to $1.7 billion (equivalent to an annual increase of 75.8 percent, based on inflation-adjusted dollars). By contrast, in the following three-year period, the annual constant-dollar growth rate fell to 14.2 percent. The machinery industry, on the other hand, grew at fairly uniform growth rates during the two periods — 9.6 percent in the 1981–1983 period, declining slightly to 8.4 percent during the ensuing period.

Department of Commerce gross investment data were not available for the years 1987 and 1988 at the time of this study, but on the basis of our analysis, we believe that growth rates in Virginia in these years rebounded from the depressed figures in the 1984–1986 period. After January 1987, for example, three of the 20 companies we studied announced or constructed facilities that will increase investments in the chemical segment by $50 million (an industry increase in Virginia of 2.5 percent over 1986) and investments in the machinery segment by $175 million (an industry increase of 79.2 percent).

The map in Figure A.3 shows the annual growth rates for gross investments of foreign manufacturing affiliates in each of the 50 states during the 1978–1986 period. As shown, Virginia was the only eastern state to maintain an annual growth rate in excess of 20 percent for investments by foreign affiliates in all industries. Other states with growth rates exceeding 20 percent were Arizona, Colorado, New Mexico, Nevada, and Texas.

Annual constant dollar growth rates of Virginia affiliates in all industries as given in Table A.1 indicate that such Virginia investments grew at a faster rate than investments in the United States as a whole and faster than investments in the five-state Southeast Atlantic region. The growth rates were 19.5 percent for Virginia, 15.0 percent for the United States, and 13.5 percent for the Southeast Atlantic states.

Figure A-4 shows, by state, the nominal-dollar capital additions of foreign manufacturing affiliates in the years 1978 through 1986. Thus, this map is a graphic indicator of the states and regions where foreign investment growth occurred during the nine-year period. Seven states — California, Illinois, Louisiana, New Jersey, Ohio, Pennsylvania, and Texas — had nominal–dollar additions of $3.0 billion or more between 1977 and 1986 ($3,000 million on the map).

Figure A.5 gives the 1986 balance of total gross investment for foreign manufacturing affiliates. Investments exceeded $4.0 billion ($4,000 million on the map) in nine states — the seven leading states in capital additions noted above, plus New York and North Carolina.

Table A.1

**GROSS BOOK VALUE AND GROWTH RATES
OF PLANT, PROPERTY, AND EQUIPMENT (GROSS INVESTMENT)
OF FOREIGN AFFILIATES**

**United States, Southeast Atlantic Region, and Virginia
Selected Years and Periods, 1977 through 1986**

	GROSS INVESTMENT ($1 Million) *Nominal* Dollars			
ALL INDUSTRIES	1977	1980	1983	1986
United States	$66,785	$127,838	$244,012	$317,607
Southeast Atlantic Region	7,311	13,035	24,331	31,085
Virginia	824	1,423	4,126	5,529
MANUFACTURING INDUSTRIES				
United States	$24,151	$46,793	$92,445	$112,995
Southeast Atlantic Region	4,424	7,432	13,578	15,236
Virginia				
Total Manufacturing	345	611	2,294	2,756
Food and Kindred Products	10	26	59	47
Chemicals and Allied Products	162	270	1,704	2,002
Primary and Fabricated Metals	23	37	129	126
Machinery and Equipment	63	110	168	221
Other Manufacturing	87	168	235	361

Table A.1 (continued)

	ANNUAL GROWTH RATES Growth in *Nominal* Dollars (Percent per Year)				ANNUAL GROWTH RATES Growth in *Constant* Dollars (Percent per Year)			
	Nine-Year Period	Three-Year Periods			Nine-Year Period	Three-Year Periods		
	1978 through 1986	1978 through 1980	1981 through 1983	1984 through 1986	1978 through 1986	1978 through 1980	1981 through 1983	1984 through 1986
ALL INDUSTRIES								
United States	18.9%	24.2%	24.0%	9.2%	15.0%	19.4%	18.0%	8.0%
Southeast Atlantic Region	17.4	21.3	23.1	8.5	13.5	16.6	17.1	7.3
Virginia	23.6	20.0	42.6	10.2	19.5	15.4	35.7	9.0
MANUFACTURING INDUSTRIES								
United States	18.7%	24.7%	25.5%	6.9%	14.8%	19.9%	19.4%	5.7%
Southeast Atlantic Region	14.7	18.9	21.7	4.4	10.9	14.3	15.8	3.3
Virginia								
Total Manufacturing	26.0	21.0	55.4	6.5	21.9	16.3	47.9	5.3
Food and Kindred Products	18.8	37.5	31.4	(7.3)	14.9	32.2	25.0	(6.1)
Chemicals and Allied Products	32.2	18.6	84.8	15.5	27.8	14.0	75.8	14.2
Primary and Fabricated Metals	20.8	17.2	51.6	(0.8)	16.8	12.7	44.2	(0.3)
Machinery and Equipment	15.0	20.4	15.2	9.6	11.2	15.8	9.6	8.4
Other Manufacturing	17.1	24.5	11.8	15.4	13.2	19.7	6.4	14.1

Note: Southeast Atlantic Region includes Maryland, Virginia, North Carolina, South Carolina, and Georgia. 1986 data are preliminary estimates. Acquisition of stock in E.I. duPont de Nemours was the major factor in the 1981-83 increase in gross investment for chemicals and allied products in Virginia.

Source: U.S. Department of Commerce, Bureau of Economic Analysis. *Foreign Direct Investment in the United States: Operations of U.S. Affiliates of Foreign Companies,* (1977-80, Revised 1983 Estimates, and Preliminary 1986 Estimates).

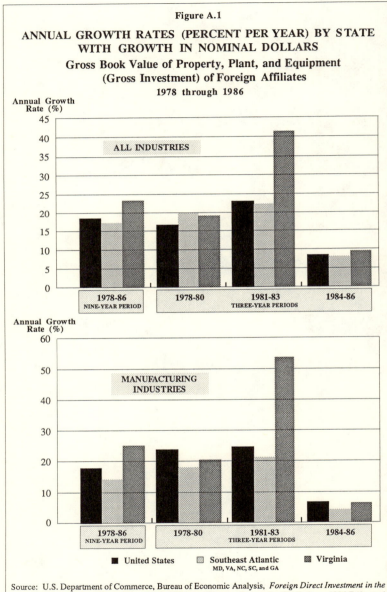

Figure A.1

ANNUAL GROWTH RATES (PERCENT PER YEAR) BY STATE WITH GROWTH IN NOMINAL DOLLARS
Gross Book Value of Property, Plant, and Equipment (Gross Investment) of Foreign Affiliates
1978 through 1986

Source: U.S. Department of Commerce, Bureau of Economic Analysis, *Foreign Direct Investment in the United States: Operations of U.S. Affiliates of Foreign Companies (Preliminary 1986 Estimates).*

126

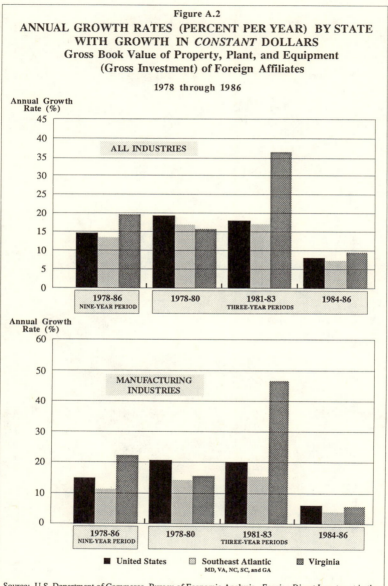

Figure A.2

ANNUAL GROWTH RATES (PERCENT PER YEAR) BY STATE
WITH GROWTH IN *CONSTANT* DOLLARS
Gross Book Value of Property, Plant, and Equipment
(Gross Investment) of Foreign Affiliates

1978 through 1986

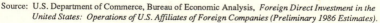

Source: U.S. Department of Commerce, Bureau of Economic Analysis, *Foreign Direct Investment in the United States: Operations of U.S. Affiliates of Foreign Companies (Preliminary 1986 Estimates).*

127

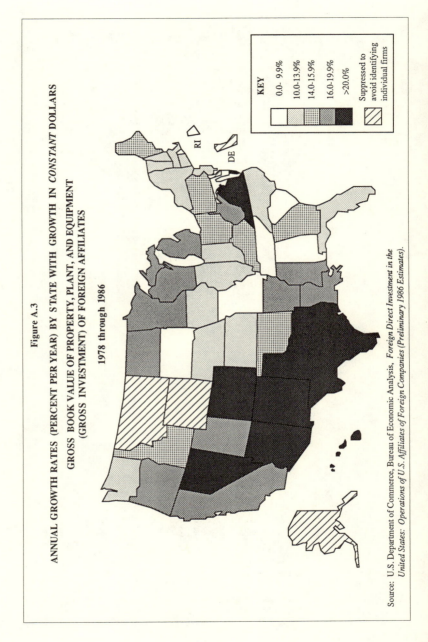

Figure A.3

ANNUAL GROWTH RATES (PERCENT PER YEAR) BY STATE WITH GROWTH IN *CONSTANT DOLLARS*

GROSS BOOK VALUE OF PROPERTY, PLANT, AND EQUIPMENT

(GROSS INVESTMENT) OF FOREIGN AFFILIATES

1978 through 1986

KEY

0.0- 9.9%
10.0-13.9%
14.0-15.9%
16.0-19.9%
>20.0%

Suppressed to
avoid identifying
individual firms

RI

DE

Source: U.S. Department of Commerce, Bureau of Economic Analysis, *Foreign Direct Investment in the*
United States: Operations of U.S. Affiliates of Foreign Companies (Preliminary 1986 Estimates).

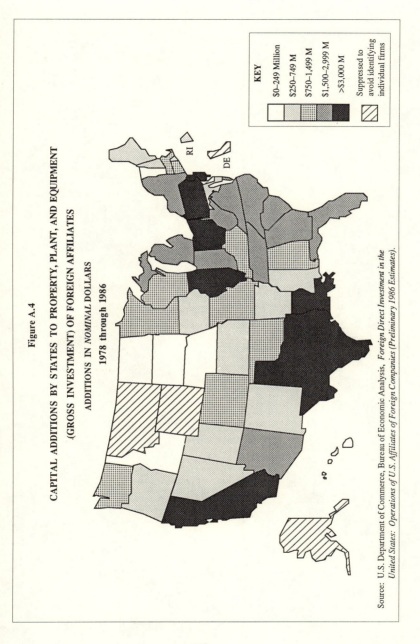

Figure A.4

CAPITAL ADDITIONS BY STATES TO PROPERTY, PLANT, AND EQUIPMENT

(GROSS INVESTMENT) OF FOREIGN AFFILIATES

ADDITIONS IN *NOMINAL* DOLLARS

1978 through 1986

KEY

$0–249 Million
$250–749 M
$750–1,499 M
$1,500–2,999 M
>$3,000 M

Suppressed to
avoid identifying
individual firms

RI
DE

Source: U.S. Department of Commerce, Bureau of Economic Analysis, *Foreign Direct Investment in the*
          United States: Operations of U.S. Affiliates of Foreign Companies (Preliminary 1986 Estimates).

Figure A.5

GROSS BOOK VALUE IN *NOMINAL DOLLARS* OF PROPERTY, PLANT, AND EQUIPMENT (GROSS INVESTMENT) OF FOREIGN AFFILIATES BY STATES

1986

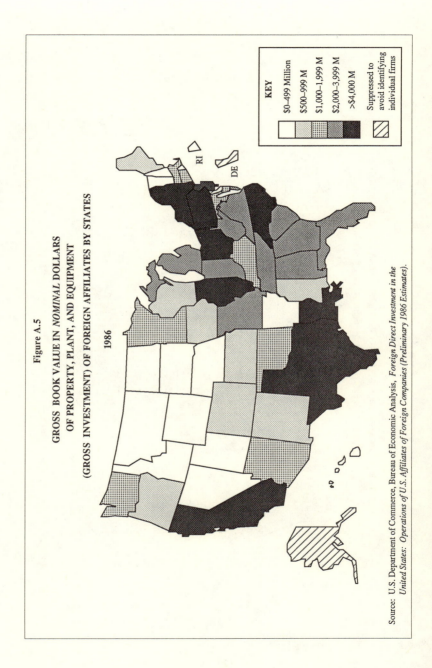

KEY

$0–499 Million
$500–999 M
$1,000–1,999 M
$2,000–3,999 M
>$4,000 M

Suppressed to
avoid identifying
individual firms

Source: U.S. Department of Commerce, Bureau of Economic Analysis, *Foreign Direct Investment in the United States: Operations of U.S. Affiliates of Foreign Companies (Preliminary 1986 Estimates).*

HOME COUNTRIES OF PARENT COMPANIES

Figure A.6 shows the percentage of total gross investments broken down by the home countries of parent companies. Breakdowns are given for three geographic areas—the United States, the five–state Southeast Atlantic region, and Virginia. In each area, the biggest change from 1977 to 1986 was the increase in ownership by Canadian companies. The increase was most striking in Virginia, where the gross investment owned by Canadians jumped from 4.6 percent of total foreign investment in 1977 to 35.9 percent in 1986.

In view of the publicity associated with recent Virginia investments by Japanese companies, readers may be surprised that Japan's percentage of gross investment in Virginia actually decreased in the period from 1977 to 1986. Although the actual dollar value of Japanese gross book value rose, as shown in Table A.2, the increases from other countries were even greater, causing Japan's percentage of the total to decrease. In 1986 the data for selected southeast Atlantic states were suppressed by the Department of Commerce to avoid the disclosure of data on individual companies.

NUMBER OF FOREIGN AFFILIATES

As shown in Table A.3, the number of foreign affiliates in the United States grew from 3,827 in 1977 to 9,669 in 1986, an annual growth rate of 10.8 percent. In the southeast Atlantic region, the number of affiliates grew from 1,141 to 2,982, an 11.3 percent annual increase. The growth of foreign affiliates from 230 to 560 in Virginia represents an annual change of 10.4 percent. Thus, the annual growth rates for the United States, the southeast Atlantic region, and Virginia are strikingly similar. The increases reported in Table A.3 include start–ups by new affiliates, additional facilities opened by existing affiliates, and additions resulting from acquisitions, mergers, and joint ventures. Our study of 20 companies included one or more cases of each of these types of business growth except for acquisitions and mergers, which were deliberately excluded for reasons cited in Part 1.

EMPLOYMENT IN FOREIGN AFFILIATES

Total employment in all industries (manufacturing and other) by foreign affiliates in Virginia grew from 23,814 in 1977 to 76,170 in 1986, an average annual increase of 13.8 percent (see Table A.4). For the United States as a whole, total employment in all industries by foreign affiliates grew from 1.219 million to 2.964 million (annual growth rate of 10.4 percent). In the manufacturing sector alone, Virginia's annual growth rate of 11.7 percent topped both the annual rate of 8.3 percent for the United States and the annual rate of 7.7 percent for five southeast

Atlantic states.

As shown in Table A.5, the percentage of total U.S. civilian, nongovernment employment represented by employment in foreign affiliates doubled from 1977 to 1986, growing from 1.5 percent of total employment to 3.0 percent. Nearly 3 million Americans were employed in foreign affiliates. For the United States as a whole, the percentage of foreign affiliate employment in the manufacturing sector alone rose from 3.4 percent in 1977 to 7.4 percent in 1986, a total of 1.4 million employees. Thus, the relative importance of employment in foreign manufacturing affiliates is significantly greater than in the nonmanufacturing industries such as wholesaling, retailing, and service activities. In 1977 foreign affiliates accounted for 3.2 percent of the manufacturing employees in Virginia; by 1986 this figure had grown to 8.0 percent.

INVESTMENT AND EMPLOYMENT OF FOREIGN AFFILIATES BY INDUSTRY SECTOR IN VIRGINIA

Figure A.7 shows the breakdown by industries of gross investment and employment for foreign manufacturing companies in Virginia. In terms of both investment and employment, the segment of chemicals and allied products was the largest in the state in both years. Primary and fabricated metals ranked second, and food and kindred products ranked third each year. Investments in the chemical industry composed 72.6 percent of all foreign manufacturing investments and 41.5 percent of all employment in foreign-owned Virginia companies.

Figure A.6

GROSS BOOK VALUE OF PROPERTY, PLANT, AND EQUIPMENT (GROSS INVESTMENT) OF FOREIGN AFFILIATES BY HOME COUNTRIES OF PARENTS

SHOWN AS A PERCENT OF TOTAL INVESTMENT — ALL INDUSTRIES, 1977 AND 1986

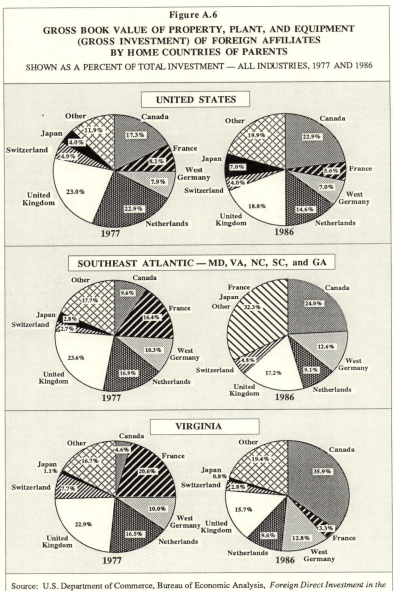

Source: U.S. Department of Commerce, Bureau of Economic Analysis, *Foreign Direct Investment in the United States: Operations of U.S. Affiliates of Foreign Companies (Preliminary 1986 Estimates).*

Table A.2

GROSS BOOK VALUE AND GROWTH RATES
OF PLANT, PROPERTY, AND EQUIPMENT (GROSS INVESTMENT)
OF FOREIGN AFFILIATES BY HOME COUNTRY OF PARENT
(ALL INDUSTRIES)

UNITED STATES, SOUTHEAST ATLANTIC REGION, AND VIRGINIA

Selected Years and Periods, 1977 through 1986

HOME COUNTRIES OF UNITED STATES FOREIGN AFFILIATES	GROSS INVESTMENT ($ million)				ANNUAL GROWTH RATES (Percent Per Year)			
					Nine-Year Period	Three-Year Periods		
	1977	1980	1983	1986	1978 through 1986	1978 through 1980	1981 through 1983	1984 through 1986
CANADA	$11,582	$23,141	$61,928	$72,685	22.6%	25.9%	38.8%	5.5%
FRANCE	5,387	9,936	14,682	17,851	14.2	22.6	13.9	6.7
WEST GERMANY	5,316	14,605	22,042	22,299	17.3	40.1	14.7	0.4
NETHERLANDS	15,260	28,376	38,250	46,493	13.2	23.0	10.5	6.7
UNITED KINGDOM	15,341	24,619	47,187	59,756	16.3	17.1	24.2	8.2
SWITZERLAND	3,261	6,807	10,110	13,392	17.0	27.8	14.1	9.8
JAPAN	2,691	5,287	10,892	22,319	26.5	25.2	27.2	27.0
OTHER	7,947	15,067	38,921	62,812	25.8	23.8	37.2	17.3
UNITED STATES TOTAL	$66,785	$127,838	$244,012	$317,607	18.9%	24.2%	24.0%	9.2%

Table A.2 (continued) **HOME COUNTRIES OF SOUTHEAST ATLANTIC FOREIGN AFFILIATES**

CANADA	$ 698	$ 1,392	$ 4,800	$ 7,454	30.1%	25.9%	51.1%	15.8%
FRANCE	1,196	1,623	(D)	(D)	(D)	10.7	(D)	(D)
WEST GERMANY	754	2,352	3,120	3,925	20.1	46.1	9.9	8.0
NETHERLANDS	1,234	1,945	2,946	2,819	9.6	16.4	14.8	(1.5)
UNITED KINGDOM	1,729	2,697	3,948	5,340	13.3	16.0	13.5	10.6
SWITZERLAND	199	494	931	1,486	25.0	35.4	23.5	16.9
JAPAN	202	327	1,033	(D)	(D)	17.4	46.7	(D)
OTHER	1,299	2,205	(D)	(D)	(D)	19.3	(D)	(D)
SOUTHEAST ATLANTIC TOTAL	$7,311	$13,035	$24,331	$31,085	17.4%	21.3%	23.1%	8.5%

HOME COUNTRIES OF VIRGINIA FOREIGN AFFILIATES

CANADA	$ 38	$ 107	$ 1,562	$ 1,986	55.2%	41.2%	144.4%	8.3%
FRANCE	170	182	177	183	0.8	2.3	(0.9)	1.1
WEST GERMANY	82	317	591	707	27.0	56.9	23.1	6.2
NETHERLANDS	136	147	350	531	16.3	2.6	33.5	14.9
UNITED KINGDOM	189	367	604	866	18.4	24.8	18.1	12.8
SWITZERLAND	63	72	125	136	8.9	4.6	20.2	2.9
JAPAN	8	17	34	48	22.0	28.6	26.0	12.2
OTHER	138	214	683	1,072	25.6	15.7	47.2	16.2
VIRGINIA TOTAL	$ 824	$ 1,423	$ 4,126	$ 5,529	23.6%	20.0%	42.6%	10.2%

Note: *Other* includes Australia, New Zealand, Latin America, the Middle East, Africa, and other Asian nations. Southeast Atlantic Region includes Maryland, Virginia, North Carolina, South Carolina, and Georgia. (D) indicates data are supressed to avoid disclosing individual companies.

Source: U.S. Department of Commerce, Bureau of Economic Analysis. *Foreign Direct Investment in the United States: Operations of U.S. Affiliates of Foreign Companies*, (1977-80, *Revised 1983 Estimates, and Preliminary 1986 Estimates*).

135

Table A.3

NUMBER OF FOREIGN AFFILIATES HAVING PLANT, PROPERTY, AND EQUIPMENT (GROSS INVESTMENT) AND GROWTH RATES

UNITED STATES, SOUTHEAST ATLANTIC REGION, AND VIRGINIA

Selected Years and Periods, 1977 through 1986

| | NUMBER OF FOREIGN AFFILIATES | | | | ANNUAL GROWTH RATES (Percent Per Year) | | | |
| | | | | | Nine-Year Period | Three-Year Periods | | |
	1977	1980	1983	1986	1978 through 1986	1978 through 1980	1981 through 1983	1984 through 1986
UNITED STATES								
CANADA	581	1,103	1,285	1,324	9.6%	23.8%	5.2%	1.0%
FRANCE	219	376	449	483	9.2	19.7	6.1	2.5
WEST GERMANY	510	981	1,230	1,305	11.0	24.4	7.8	2.0
NETHERLANDS	150	347	446	442	12.8	32.3	8.7	(0.3)
UNITED KINGDOM	430	632	933	1,087	10.9	13.7	13.9	5.2
SWITZERLAND	266	585	727	761	12.4	30.0	7.5	1.5
JAPAN	545	680	767	902	5.8	7.7	4.1	5.6
OTHER	1,126	2,118	3,023	3,365	12.9	23.4	12.6	3.6
UNITED STATES TOTAL	3,827	6,822	8,860	9,669	10.8%	21.3%	9.1%	3.0%

Table A.3 (continued)

SOUTHEAST ATLANTIC REGION

CANADA	163	246	289	325	8.0%	14.7%	5.5%	4.0%
FRANCE	97	152	159	168	6.3	16.2	1.5	1.9
WEST GERMANY	176	365	496	537	17.6	42.9	10.8	2.7
NETHERLANDS	73	149	220	202	9.3	17.9	13.9	(2.8)
UNITED KINGDOM	179	337	470	547	13.2	23.5	11.7	5.2
SWITZERLAND	82	172	219	232	12.2	28.0	8.4	1.9
JAPAN	96	147	210	245	11.0	15.3	12.6	5.3
OTHER	275	417	588	726	10.0	10.6	12.1	7.3
SOUTHEAST ATLANTIC TOTAL	1,141	1,985	2,651	2,982	11.3%	20.3%	10.1%	4.0%

VIRGINIA

CANADA	28	44	58	64	9.6%	16.3%	9.6%	3.3%
FRANCE	26	47	48	39	4.6	21.8	0.7	(6.7)
WEST GERMANY	38	58	80	83	9.1	15.1	11.3	1.2
NETHERLANDS	14	32	43	39	12.1	31.7	10.4	(3.2)
UNITED KINGDOM	34	69	92	102	13.0	26.6	10.1	3.5
SWITZERLAND	23	28	45	42	6.9	6.8	17.1	(2.3)
JAPAN	9	15	19	24	11.5	18.6	8.2	8.1
OTHER	58	95	130	167	12.5	17.9	11.0	8.7
VIRGINIA TOTAL	230	388	515	560	10.4%	19.0%	9.9%	2.8%

Note: *Other* includes Australia, New Zealand, Latin America, the Middle East, Africa, and other Asian nations. Southeast Atlantic Region includes Maryland, Virginia, North Carolina, South Carolina, and Georgia.

Source: U.S. Department of Commerce, Bureau of Economic Analysis. *Foreign Direct Investment in the United States: Operations of U.S. Affiliates of Foreign Companies, (1977-80, Revised 1983 Estimates, and Preliminary 1986 Estimates).*

Table A.4

EMPLOYMENT IN FOREIGN AFFILIATES AND GROWTH RATES
UNITED STATES, SOUTHEAST ATLANTIC REGION, AND VIRGINIA

Selected Years and Periods, 1977 through 1986

| | NUMBER OF EMPLOYEES (thousand) | | | | ANNUAL GROWTH RATES (Percent Per Year) | | | |
| | | | | | Nine-Year Period | Three-Year Periods | | |
	1977	1980	1983	1986	1978 through 1986	1978 through 1986	1978 through 1986	1978 through 1986
ALL INDUSTRIES								
United States	1,219	2,034	2,547	2,964	10.4%	18.6%	7.8%	5.2%
Southeast Atlantic Region	157	267	345	419	11.5	19.5	8.9	6.6
Virginia	24	37	57	76	13.8	16.0	15.0	10.4
MANUFACTURING INDUSTRIES								
United States	686	1,105	1,321	1,400	8.3%	17.2%	6.1%	1.9%
Southeast Atlantic Region	104	147	190	203	7.7	12.1	8.9	2.3
Virginia								
Total Manufacturing	13	16	33	34	11.7	7.4	28.4	1.0
Food and Kindred Products	2	2	3	2	3.0	6.0	12.0	(8.0)
Chemicals and Allied Products	2	3	14	14	23.0	11.1	65.8	0.9
Primary and Fabricated Metals	2	2	6	5	12.6	4.3	44.8	(5.5)
Machinery and Equipment	4	4	5	5	3.3	6.2	7.4	(3.3)
Other Manufacturing	3	4	5	7	10.1	10.3	3.4	17.1

Note: Southeast Atlantic Region includes Maryland, Virginia, North Carolina, South Carolina, and Georgia. 1986 data are preliminary estimates. Acquisition of stock in E.I. duPont de Nemours was the major factor in the 1981-83 increase in gross investment for chemicals and allied products in Virginia.

Source: U.S. Department of Commerce, Bureau of Economic Analysis. *Foreign Direct Investment in the United States: Operations of U.S. Affiliates of Foreign Companies*, (1977-80, Revised 1983 Estimates, and Preliminary 1986 Estimates).

Table A.5

EMPLOYMENT OF FOREIGN AFFILIATES
and
CIVILIAN NONAGRICULTURAL WORK FORCE

1977 and 1986

| | NUMBER OF EMPLOYEES (thousand) | | | | EMPLOYEES IN FOREIGN AFFILIATES Percent of Total | |
| | Foreign Affiliates | | Civilian Nonagricultural Work Force | | | |
	1977	1986	1977	1986	1977	1986
ALL INDUSTRIES						
United States	1,219	2,964	82,256	99,610	1.5%	3.0%
Virginia	24	76	1,931	2,557	1.2	3.0
MANUFACTURING INDUSTRIES						
United States	686	1,400	19,984	18,994	3.4%	7.4%
Virginia	13	34	401	424	3.2	8.0

Sources: United States Department of Commerce, Bureau of Economic Analysis. *Foreign Direct Investment in the United States: Operations of U.S. Affiliates of Foreign Companies, (1977–80 and Prelminary 1986 Estimates).*
United States Department of Commerce, Bureau of the Census, *Statistical Abstract of the United States, 1978 and 1988.*

Figure A.7

GROSS BOOK VALUE OF PROPERTY, PLANT, AND EQUIPMENT (GROSS INVESTMENT) AND EMPLOYMENT OF FOREIGN AFFILIATES

SELECTED MANUFACTURING INDUSTRIES IN VIRGINIA AS A PERCENT OF VIRGINIA TOTAL

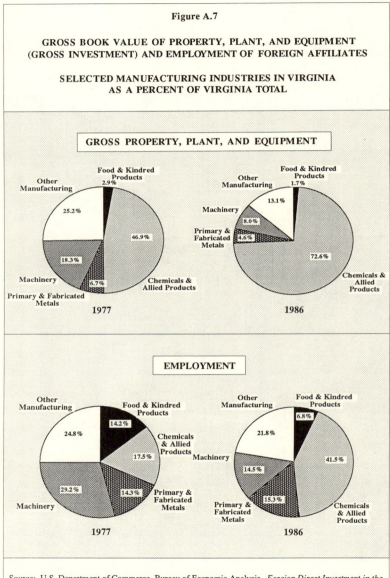

Source: U.S. Department of Commerce, Bureau of Economic Analysis, *Foreign Direct Investment in the United States: Operations of U.S. Affiliates of Foreign Companies (Preliminary 1986 Estimates).*

BIBLIOGRAPHY

Aharoni, Yair. *The Foreign Investment Decision Process*. Boston: Harvard University, 1966.

Ajami, Riad A. and R. BarNiv. "Utilizing Economic Indicators in Explaining Foreign Direct Investment in the U.S." *Management International Review* 24 (1984): 16–26.

Ajami, Riad A. and David A. Ricks." Motives of Foreign Firms Investing in the U.S.", *Journal of International Business Studies* 12 (Winter, 1981): 25–34.

Arpan, Jeffrey S. "The Impact of State Incentives on Foreign Investors' Site Selections." *Federal Reserve Bank of Atlanta Economic Review* 66 (December, 1981): 36–42.

Blair, John P. and Robert Premus. "Major Factors in Industrial Location: A Review." *Economic Development Quarterly* (February, 1987): 72–85.

Calvet, A. L. "A Synthesis of Foreign Direct Investment Theories and Theories of the Multinational Firm." *Journal of International Business Studies* 12 (Spring/ Summer, 1981): 43–59.

Carroll, Thomas. "Right-to-Work Laws Do Matter." *Southern Economic Journal* 50 (October, 1983): 494–509.

Caves, Richard. "Causes of Direct Investment: Foreign Firms' Share in Canadian and United Kingdom Manufacturing Industries." *Review of Economics and Statistics* 56 (August, 1974): 279–293.

Caves, Richard. "Corporations: The International Industrial Economics of Foreign Investment." *Economica* 38 (February, 1971): 1–27.

Chernotsky, H. I. "Selecting U.S. Sites: A Case Study of German and Japanese Firms." *Management International Review* 23 (1983): 45–55.

"Conway Data Survey, Geo-Political Index." *Industrial Development and Site Selection Handbook* (now *Site Selection and Industrial Development*) (October, 1985 and October, 1986): 1008–1014.

Daniels, John. *Recent Foreign Direct Investment in the United States*. New York: Praeger, 1971.

Davidson, W. H. "The Location of Foreign Direct Investment Activity, Country Characteristics and Experience Effect." *Journal of International Business Studies* 11 (Fall, 1980): 9–22.

Dunning, John H. "Toward an Eclectic Theory of International Production: Some Empirical Tests." *Journal of International Business Studies* 11 (Spring/Summer, 1980): 9–31.

Flowers, Edward Brown. "Oligopolistic Reactions in European and Canadian Direct Investment in the United States." *Journal of International Business Studies* 7 (Fall/Winter, 1976): 43–55.

Franko, Lawrence G. *The European Multinationals*. Stamford: Greylock Press, 1976.

Graham, Edward. "Transatlantic Investment by Multinational Firms: A Rivalistic Phenomenon?" *Journal of Post-Keynesian Economics* 1 (1978): 82–99.

Grant Thornton. *Ninth Annual Grant Thornton Manufacturing Climates Study*. Englewood Cliffs, N.J.: Prentice-Hall, July 1988.

Green, R. T. and Cunningham, W. H. "The Determinants of U.S. Foreign Investment: An Empirical Examination." *Management International Review* 15, No. 2/3 (1975): 113–120.

Grubaugh, S. G. "Determinants of Direct Foreign Investment." *Review of Economics and Statistics* (February, 1987): 149–151.

Hack, G. D. "The Plant Location Decision Making Process." *Industrial Development* 153 (September/October, 1984): 31–33.

Hekman, John S. "What Are Businesses Looking For?" *Federal Reserve Bank of Atlanta Economic Review* 67 (June, 1982): 6–19.

Horst, T. O. "Firm and Industry Determinants of the Decision to Invest Abroad." *Review of Economics and Statistics* 54 (August, 1972): 258–266.

Hymer, Stephen H. *The International Operations of National Firms: A Study of Direct Foreign Investment.* Cambridge, Massachusetts: MIT Press, 1976.

Kahley, William J. "Direct Investment Activity of Foreign Firms." *Federal Reserve Bank of Atlanta Economic Review* 72 (Summer, 1987): 36–51.

Kahley, William J. "What's Behind Patterns of State Job Growth?" *Federal Reserve Bank of Atlanta Economic Review* 71 (May, 1986): 4–18.

Kim, Wi Saeng and Esmeralda O. Lyn. "Foreign Investment Theories, Entry Barriers and Reverse Investments in U.S. Manufacturing Industries." *Journal of International Business Studies* 18 (Summer, 1987): 53–66.

Kindleberger, Charles P. *American Business Abroad.* New Haven: Yale University Press, 1969.

Knickerbocker, F. T. *Oligopolistic Reaction and Multinational Enterprise.* Cambridge, Massachusetts: Harvard University Press, 1974.

Lall, Sanjaya and N. S. Siddharthan. "The Monopolistic Advantages of Multinationals: Lessons from Foreign Investment in the United States." *The Economic Journal* 92 (September, 1982): 668–683.

Little, Jane Sneddon. "The Industrial Composition of Foreign Direct Investment in the U.S. and Abroad: A Preliminary Look." *New England Economic Review* (May/June, 1984): 38–48.

Lumsden, Keith and Craig Peterson. "The Effect of Right-to-Work Laws on Unionization in the United States." *Journal of Political Economy* 83 (December, 1975): 1237–1248.

McClain, David. *Foreign Direct Investment in the United States: Old Currents, New Waves and the Theory of Direct Investment in the Multinational Corporation in the 1980s.* Edited by C. P. Kindleberger and D. A. Audretsch. Cambridge: MIT Press, 1983.

Markusen, James R. "Multinationals, Multiplant Economies, and the Gains from Trade." *Journal of International Economics* 3/4, (May, 1984): 205–226.

Moore, William J. and Robert J. Newman. "The Effects of Right-to-Work Laws: A Review of the Literature." *Industrial and Labor Relations Review* 38 (July, 1985): 571–585.

Morrow, Robert. "Direct Foreign Investment in the United States: Investment Motivation." *Federal Reserve Bank of Atlanta Economic Review* 25 (September/October, 1975): 21–25.

O'Connor, Michael. "Officials' Ratings, Local Improvements Underscore Importance of Quality of Life." *Industrial Development and Site Selection Handbook* (now *Site Selection and Industrial Development*) (August, 1987): 778–784.

Pittman, Robert H. "Economic Development Organizations Provide Information Useful to Investors." *Industrial Development and Site Selection Handbook* (now *Site Selection and Industrial Development*) (August, 1985): 8–13.

Renner, G. T. "Geography of Industrial Localization." *Economic Geography* 23 (1947): 167–189.

Rugman, Alan M. *New Theories of the Multinational Enterprise*. New York: St. Martin, 1983.

Scaperlanda, A. E. and L. T. Mauer. "The Determinants of U.S. Direct Investment in the EEC." *American Economic Review* 59 (September, 1969): 558–568.

Schmenner, Roger W. *Making Business Location Decisions*. Englewood Cliffs, New Jersey: Prentice-Hall, Inc., 1982.

Schmenner, Roger W., Joel Huber, and Randal Cook. "Geographic Differences and the Location of New Manufacturing Facilities." *Journal of Urban Economics* 21 (January, 1987): 83–104.

Severn, Alan K. and Martin M. Lawrence. "Direct Investment, Research Intensity, and Profitability." *Journal of Financial Quantitative Analysis* 9 (March, 1974): 181–193.

Stafford, H. A. *Principles of Industrial Facility Location*. Atlanta, Georgia: Conway Publications, Inc., 1980.

Tolchin, Martin and Susan Tolchin. *Buying into America: How Foreign Money is Changing the Face of Our Nation*. New York: Times Books, 1988.

Tong, Hsin-Min. *Plant Location Decisions of Foreign Manufacturing Investors*. Ann Arbor, Michigan: UMI Research Press, 1979.

U.S. Department of Commerce. Bureau of the Census. *National Data Book and Guide to Sources: Statistical Abstract of the United States*, 1988.

U.S. Department of Commerce. "The Determinants of Foreign Direct Investment in the U.S." *Survey of Current Business* (February, 1973): 35.

U.S. Department of Commerce. *Foreign Direct Investment in the U.S. Vol. 5, Investment Motivation*. Washington, D.C.: GPO, 1986.

U.S. Department of Commerce. Bureau of Economic Analysis. *Foreign Direct Investment in the United States: Operations of U.S. Affiliates.* Washington, D.C.: GPO, 1977–1986.

U.S. Department of Commerce. International Trade Administration. Office of Trade and Investment Analysis. *Foreign Direct Investment in the United States: Completed Transactions, 1974–1983.* Washington, D.C.: GPO, 1977–1985.

U.S. Department of Commerce. International Trade Administration. Office of Trade and Investment Analysis. *Foreign Direct Investment in the United States: 1985 Transactions.* Washington, D.C.: GPO, 1986.

U.S. Department of Commerce. International Trade Administration. Office of Trade and Investment Analysis. *Foreign Direct Investment in the United States: 1986 Transactions.* Washington, D.C.: GPO, 1987.

Virginia Department of Economic Development and Department of Planning and Budget. *Economic Development Activities in Virginia and Other States,* December, 1986.

Wardrep, B. N. "Factors Which Play Major Roles in Location Decisions." *Industrial Development* 154 (July/August,1985): 8–12.

INDEX

ABOUT THE AUTHORS

Robert W. Haigh is Distinguished Professor of Business Administration at the University of Virginia's Darden Graduate School of Business Administration and is associated with the School's Tayloe Murphy International Business Studies Center, under whose auspices the present work was written.

In addition to his Darden School experience, where Dr. Haigh served as Dean, he was on the faculties of the Wharton School at the University of Pennsylvania, where he was Director of the Wharton Applied Research Center, and the Harvard Business School, where he taught and co-authored *The Growth of Integrated Oil Companies.*

As an industry executive Dr. Haigh was Vice President for Planning and Corporate Development at The Standard Oil Company (Ohio) and President of Sohio's Chemicals and Plastics subsidiaries. He served as a Group Vice President and Director of Xerox Corporation, where he was responsible for corporate development and technology acquisition. At Xerox, Dr. Haigh was also President of the Educational Publishing Group. In other industry assignments, he was President and CEO of Swedlow, Inc., Senior Vice President, Planning and Development of Freeport-McMoran, Inc., and Financial Vice President of Helmerich & Payne, Inc.

Dr. Haigh specializes in strategy formulation and the management of corporate development, new business development, and R&D commercial development projects. He conducted negotiations with European and Asian business managers and had the general management responsibility for operating subsidiaries headquartered in Europe and Australia.

Teresa K. Welch is a full-time research assistant at the Tayloe Murphy International Business Studies Center, and Richard A. Adams and Clark F. Driftmier were students at the Darden School who also assumed research assistant responsibilities at the Center.